W9-CFK-762

A FAMILY OF EAGLES

A FAMILY OF EAGLES

Dan True

EVEREST HOUSE

Publishers · *New York*

Library of Congress Cataloging in Publication Data:
True, Dan, 1924–
   A family of eagles.
   1. Golden eagle.—Behavior   I. Title
QL696.F32T78   1980   598'.916   79-28216
ISBN: 0-89696-078-1

Copyright © 1980 by Dan True
All Rights Reserved
Published simultaneously in Canada by
Beaverbooks, Pickering, Ontario
Manufactured in the United States of America
Designed by Joyce Cameron Weston
First Edition FG780

To Greg, who should have
lived longer

A FAMILY OF EAGLES

I

GRASSY PRAIRIE FORMS THE ORIGIN of a hundred-mile canyon gouged from plains of the Texas panhandle. The canyon's beginning is simple enough: a series of trenches, converging into a common, deeper cut. Within a mile, erosion has chiseled the cut to gulch size. Another mile on, the gulch becomes an adolescent canyon, where water bleeds from the deepening gash. Suddenly, the gorge plunges seven hundred feet below the prairie and spans a mile. Known as Palo Duro Canyon, it geologically fits atop the Grand, and takes its name from Kiowa Indian words meaning *hard wood*.

To go back briefly in history, in 1877, Colonel Charles Goodnight established the first ranch in the Palo Duro. Other settlers followed, and ensuing progress changed most of the gorge. Now, its middle segment has been transformed from Goodnight ranchland into a state park, with the colonel's first dugout preserved there, amid paving, tourist facilities, and concession stands. Seven miles above the park, however, in the rugged heart of Palo Duro Canyon, lays the sixteen-thousand acre Currie Ranch. Here, only eighteen miles southeast of Amarillo, time and progress have paused. With a terrain too formidable for modern roads, this land has escaped that pressure. The estate remains as it was in 2000 B.C. Here, the canyon is hushed enough for the red wolf to pad silently through cedar-forested game trails; remote enough for deer to browse in peace; and tranquil enough for the eagle to live and to nest.

9

It was a soft April evening, the start of my third week living on Currie Ranch. A short distance to my right lay the rim of Palo Duro Canyon. In front of me, and my movie camera, a herd of tan and white pronghorn antelope munched along under the watchful eye of "daddy buck." Approaching sunset had painted an artist's sky of chiffon pinks and blues. Anticipating unusually colorful film, I made adjustments to my camera and was ready to start its motor when a diving eagle sliced into my right-side vision.

Basically, I am the weatherman for an Amarillo television station. Additionally, I produce and narrate a weekly wildlife show called "True Nature." To tell the truth, I probably do TV weather to support my wildlife filming. Although I think I'm not a nature nut, I do like the outdoors. The speeding eagle's wings harped in the wind. I raised my binoculars to the chocolate brown bird.

The eagle had drawn its wings into a delta. Its speed was probably a hundred miles per hour, and its flight was serious, as though after something. I moved my glasses to scan the ground ahead of the eagle's track. A jackrabbit was tearing across the land, zigging and zagging raising puffs of dust at each turn. It probably wasn't amusing to the bunny, but its desperation had a comical air. The eagle rapidly closed in. From just behind the rabbit, the bird spread its wings, checking its speed to perhaps fifty. Coming into range of the rabbit, the eagle rotated and brought its talons forward, into what I presumed was rabbit-grabbing position. I sensed the rabbit's moment of truth had arrived and felt sorry for the gray and white rodent. Instead of grabbing, however, the eagle made fists of its talons and punched at the speeding rabbit's head.

A whisker ahead of the eagle's savage punch, the rabbit bolted right, half-skidded, regained footing, and raced away. The big bird banked sharply right, but its speed was spent, and it could do little more than awkwardly flap after the accelerating rabbit.

The rabbit scampered down into a shallow draw and dove head-long into a green cedar bush. The bush was five or six feet in diameter and about eight feet high.

The eagle climbed toward the bush. As the bird rose over the tree, a second, larger eagle lumbered into view. This bird was descending and it quickly landed on the ground beside the tree. By its larger size, I identified the second eagle as female, because I had learned female prey birds are larger than their mates. That strange fact had stirred my curiosity. I also noted this bird was missing a right wing feather. The climbing male, or tiercel, mounted higher in the Texas sky, to about a hundred feet above the cedar. Here, he circled. The female then spread her wings, waddled to the cedar, and with opened, hissing beak, flogged the bush. She walked awkwardly on her taloned feet, as a novice on skis. The rabbit nonchalantly hopped to a different side of the bush.

The hen eagle waddled around the bush and flogged a second time. Again, the rabbit shifted location. After another walk, flog, and shift, the eagle paused and peered at the rabbit through the cedar's branches. Above the bush, the tiercel continued circling, as though waiting for the rabbit to run. After a moment of peering, the female reluctantly turned, faced into the wind, spread her wings for flight, hippety-hopped a few steps, and launched. Mentally, I scored, rabbits one, eagles zero. The two birds flew toward the line on my right that marked the land's transition from prairie to canyon. As I watched the birds flap away, I was reminded of my first and frightening experience with an eagle.

I was a half-sized fifth grader in the Rocky Mountain town of Ruidoso, New Mexico. One bright September morning, I was trudging the pine-bordered gravel road from my parents' cabin to school. Several classmates and I were joshing and giggling our way toward another day's education when one boy suddenly stopped. Pointing through the trees ahead, he yelled, "Look at that!"

"That" was a bomber-sized bird, boring straight toward us. The bird's brown wings glistened in the early sun. Its honey gold head moved from side to side, as if searching the ground below. The bird's flapping wings harped the mountain air in a low, melodious, "woosh-woosh-woosh."

"It's an eagle!" the boy shouted. As if we hadn't figured that out. The boy grabbed my arm, jerked me toward the shadow overhead, and hollered, "Hey, Mr. Eagle, want half-pint here for breakfast?"

The bird's awesome size made my skin crawl. I shrank away. The mass sailed nearer and nearer. Wide-eyed, I had the feeling if Mr. Eagle wanted me for breakfast, he could probably take me.

Another boy raised an imaginary gun, fired an imaginary charge, and snarled, "I killed the son of a bitch." His angry voice tone was startling. The eagle came on and sailed by. I broke free and continued watching, until the eagle disappeared behind pine tops. Relieved, I nevertheless felt a strange, eerie sadness, as though the eagle's departure had deprived me of something unknown. The boy who "shot" the eagle stamped the ground and clenched his fist after the bird. "Damn! If I'd only had my .30–.30." His face was contorted in a way that surprised, in fact, nearly alarmed me.

A third-grade girl marched in front of the "shooter," looked up, and shook her finger at his face. "I'm glad you didn't," she blurted, verging on tears. This girl was normally the shyest in school, and again I was surprised. Her speech made, she blushed, bowed her head, and melted back into her quietness. We walked on, jabbering about eagles.

To some of my classmates, the bird was a winged, sheep-killing demon. To others, the eagle was magical, with divine qualities deserving religious respect. The school's brain, a horn-rim-bespectacled girl, volunteered the fact that our alphabet's small *a* was derived from a side view of a sitting eagle. According to her, the top of the *a* is the bird's head and neck, the left bulge the bird's breast, and the tic at the *a*'s lower right is the eagle's tail. She was a straight-*A* student, and I suppose that's why we accepted her information as fact. After a pause, she added that the bird is a thirty-seven-million-year-old, living, prehistoric creature. Quickly then, almost as if to show off, she further added that earth's average life form survives only 2½ to 5 million years.

I started to ask how long man had been tracking the earth when the boy who grabbed my arm cracked, "Yeah, and I hear they've been carrying away small children thirty-five of those thirty-seven jillion years."

I shivered again, and the school's jokester looked at the boy and said, "Well, where were you?" Everyone laughed, and my liking for the jokester rose a notch. Within another four steps, arguments reerupted about the eagle's merits. The arguments spanned the spectrum of human emotions, and as I listened, my eagle interest soared. Before we reached school, I resolved to know more about this big brown bird called *eagle*.

Now, some thirty years later, I felt the same pull toward these fascinating creatures. As I watched the two eagles above the canyon in my binoculars, I was aware that the antelope in front of me were probably moving on and that I was missing good film. However, I couldn't stop watching the eagles. The birds were still circling, riding updraft air interfacing with the canyon rim. Suddenly, the tiercel folded his wings and dove on a red-tailed hawk sailing low along the rim. As the eagle plunged toward the hawk, I was reminded of another encounter I had had, accidentally, with a mad eagle in the sky near Ruidoso.

Several weeks after seeing the eagle on my way to school, my quest for firsthand eagle knowledge proved frustrating, so I turned to a pursuit more conventional for kids my age: kite flying. One nice afternoon, I had my handmade kite aloft over a meadow not too far from our cabin. I had given the kite full line and was studying its flight, calculating bridle or tail adjustments, when a dark speck appeared high above my treasure. The speck resembled a falling rock, but my mind dismissed that as impossible. Nevertheless, the speck made me uneasy. Then I thought, maybe it was an object that fell, or was dropped, from some airplane. Whatever, it was falling straight toward my kite. I pulled in line in arm over arm gulps. To my surprise, the object reacted by seeming to accelerate. I hauled faster, but the faster I hauled, the faster the object plummeted toward my kite. Collision turned from imminent to certain. In desperation, I ran backwards, stumbled, and frantically yanked. Suddenly, wings and yellow claws sprouted from the speck. Just as suddenly, the claws slashed through my kite's spruce spars. The kite faltered, my line went slack, and, unbelieving, I watched my flyer flutter down, a misshapen mass of broken sticks, rattling paper, and tangled tail. What I now recognized as an eagle checked its speed and flew casual circles around my tumbling wreck, looking like a fighter pilot watching a victim's death plunge. My kite crashed to earth. Apparently satisfied, the eagle turned away and disappeared into the blue, as silently as it had come.

Triumphantly, I bore the wreckage home. Friends, neighbors, and my mom exclaimed over what was left, and my eagerness for eagle knowledge flamed anew. Three days later, however, my family and I moved from New Mexico to Shelbyville, Illinois.

Above Palo Duro canyon's rim, the diving male eagle slashed its talons at the redtail. Deftly, the hawk turned away and flapped back upcanyon, where I suppose it had come from. After a short chase, the eagle turned back, spread his wings full sail, and rose once more toward the female. In the quiet of the prairie evening, it occurred to me that, after thirty-two years, a war, three thousand flying hours, and a marriage, my opportunity to know the eagle just might be at hand.

At about a thousand feet high, the eagles continued circling, at the same time slowly progressing downcanyon. The bird's flight pattern, and their moving heads, suggested they were continuing to hunt. With the sun sinking lower, the pair edged on, flying over an occasional cedar rooted on the canyon's edge. After they had gone about two miles, two additional eagles rose into the air, as if to challenge the hunting team. At the hunting eagles' altitude, the new eagles faced into the canyon above the rim and stabilized, as though waiting. The hunting pair eased on, to within a hundred yards of the new eagles. Here, they too faced into the canyon and hung motionless. The smaller of the two waiting eagles then folded his wings and made a mock attack at the hunting male. The hunter refused to flinch. At the last moment, the new, and I now assumed neighboring tiercel, turned away. I noted that the new tiercel turned in time to remain on his side of an imaginary line between the two pairs of eagles. That tweaked my curiosity. From the group's behavior, I presumed the hunting pair had reached the downcanyon limit of their territory and had been denied further progress by the neighboring pair. The territory defense prompted me to breathe, "Aha. Now I understand my kite being knocked from the sky."

In enlightenment's glow, my smile widened, my curiosity matured, and I wondered how is one to know when one has violated an eagle territory limit. "How," I whispered, "would the king of birds mark territorial limits, in thin air?"

After a moment, the hunting pair turned and flew a straight, descending track back upcanyon. When they had traveled a mile or so, sinking lower and lower, they disappeared into the canyon's diminishing light. Feeling the eagle's disappearance had again deprived me of something unknown. That same sadness I had felt as a youngster in New Mexico enveloped me. The throaty call of a nighthawk, coupled with the song of its wings slicing the evening air, brought me back to the present. Reluctantly, I lowered my binoculars and returned to the camera in front of me. The antelope had moved on half a mile or so, out of range. The sky was flame red, with touches of gray. Happy with my eagle-antelope tradeoff, I packed my gear into my tan VW and drove across the grassland, steering for Currie Ranch headquarters, on the canyon floor. Unconsciously, I knew which of the ranch's creatures I'd watch tomorrow.

II

CURRIE RANCH IS LAID OUT in an east-west rectangle, with Palo Duro Canyon slashing the spread from northwest to southwest. My home, Currie headquarters house, rests on the canyon floor. Only one unimproved road links the prairie to the canyon's depth. That road tracks north to south, along the ranch's west edge. The trail begins at the ranch's north gate, a gate that opens onto a paved road to Amarillo. From the gate, the road runs south across flat grassland sparsely studded with mesquite and yucca. Two miles from the gate, there was a prairie dog town with perhaps fifty of the little brown animals that are really prairie squirrels. (The squirrels live on roots and seeds and are as tasty as any tree squirrel cousin. In a way, it's a shame the animals were labeled prairie *dogs*. They live in ground burrows simply because there are no trees for them. Had they been accurately named, I think there would be a regular hunting season on them. Unfortunately, *dog* indicates the little critters were on man's vermin list.) Four miles from the gate, the trail squeezes through a narrow cut in the canyon rim. In my VW, I headed for that cut.

At the cut, I downshifted and steered through the steep, rocky trail. The notch's walls reverberated my engine's rumble. Past the cut, the track turns into the first of five switchbacks that stitch canyon wall to canyon floor. The trail threads through car-sized boulders, tamarack, mountain mahogany, scrub oak, yucca, clumps of love grass, and juniper. Aroma of juniper prevailed.

I braked to a stop and drew a deep breath. In the two weeks I had lived here, I had come to love the canyon: the boisterous freedom of its plunge below the prairie and the uninhibited reach of its width. My mood often flowed with cliff colors and shadows responding to the shifting sun. I enjoyed the canyon's diamond velvet nights, sometimes mist-shrouded mornings, and sometimes spirited winds. I drew another breath and rolled on.

Behind me, the canyon's wall rose. Across the way, the canyon's south wall loomed. Both are a rainbow of geological Spanish Skirts, occasionally riffled by the maw of a finger canyon joining the main gorge. Below, the canyon's deep, shadowed floor is carpeted with green grass, dotted with light green mesquite and yucca. Near the middle of the canyon, a small stream meanders, babbling through occasional cottonwood groves. By world standards, the spring is tiny, but its name is the Prairie Dog Town Fork of the Red River.

Where canyon wall meets canyon floor, the road straightens and runs across exposed, gray bedrock. Sporadic storm runoff has cut through the bedrock and has eroded earth away to a depth of sixty feet, straight down. Around the edge of the bedrock, further erosion has washed out a U-shaped basin, a hundred yards wide. To my left, that basin yawned. Behind, the basin's left edge fused with the canyon wall, forming a high cliff from prairie to stream bed. I drove on. A few feet back from where the stream falls over the bedrock's lip, my VW's tires splashed through The Prairie Dog Town Fork of the Red. From the lip, the water pours into a clear pool below. Past the stream, the trail angles away from the basin, rises onto ground known as second level, and turns back toward the cliff. From the waterfall, the basin's walls continue downstream, widening, deepening, and swinging in a bend under the cliff. On second level, I passed between a vine-covered, weathering, wooden windmill on my left, and the stable on my right. A hundred yards ahead lay Currie

Ranch headquarters, sheltered from north winds by the cliff across the deeply walled stream.

The main house is a native-stone, single-level affair. A blue-tiled pool corners off the front porch, with a bunkhouse-garage edging the north side of the pool. The compound is enclosed by a cedar stockade fence. Inside the fence, elm, walnut, and hackberry trees grow. Outside, away from the bunkhouse toward the cliff, stands a spacious chicken lot and hen house. I pulled onto the cement pad in front of the garage, parked, and stepped toward the main house. My phone was ringing and I hurried.

The call was from Douglas Grayson, of White Deer, Texas, forty-three miles northeast of Amarillo. In my travels about the panhandle, I had heard of nineteen-year-old Douglas. He was a falconer. Because he was a falconer, I didn't like him, even though we'd never met. I admit that's not bright, but that's the way I felt. But falconers, with their smug pride about subverting a wild creature's natural hunting instincts to pointless kills for their own showing off, had a remote fascination to me.

On the phone, Douglas said he had enjoyed my nature program, and was calling because he had a problem with an eagle. He had my attention. He went on to say, he was going into the army, and would I be interested in helping him return his four-year-old golden eagle to the wild. Douglas explained that since the bird was trained to hunt, it should have little difficulty adapting. Could he bring the eagle to me for its transition? he wanted to know. The chicken lot would make a perfect eagle halfway house, I thought, and answered, "Yes, sir."

"When?"

"Anytime. I'm here every day until three o'clock and all weekend."

"Tomorrow morning? Nine, or nine thirty?"

"Fine." I gave Douglas directions to the ranch, hung up, and cautioned myself to hold an open mind about falconers.

It was just after nine Sunday morning when I noticed a car ease across the bedrock, splash through the stream, and turn toward headquarters house. Assuming it was Douglas, I stepped outside.

Meadowlark song came from across the way, mourning dove cooed in a yard tree, and a cardinal flashed into hackberry beyond the bunkhouse. Scents of spring flora highlighted warming air. The car passed between windmill and stable, rolled down the trail in front of the house and onto the cement pad.

The minute I shook Douglas's hand, I felt foolish for having prejudged. He was a shy, polite, instantly likable sort, about 5'8", with blue eyes and blond hair. Although I was drawn to him personally, I still held reservations about his falconry. Without wasting time, he asked, "Would you like to meet Sandose, Mr. True?"

"Sure, and please call me Dan."

Douglas slipped on a well-worn leather glove. Over the glove went a sheepskin gauntlet that covered from glove to just short of his elbow. With loving care, he took the hooded eagle from his car, and onto his fist. The bird's feet seemed oversized; its curved black talons looked lethal. While talking to Sandose in soothing tones, Douglas threaded the bird's leather leg straps, or jesses, through his fingers, just so. Bells on the eagle's full-feathered legs jingled. The bird's body and wing feathers glistened in the sunlight. To see such magnificence in leather straps, bells, and a red hood rankled me. With the eagle secure, Douglas deftly removed its hood.

The eagle shook its head and searched its surroundings. The bird's alert eyes were amber gold, with intense black pupils. And as all prey birds appear, Sandose looked as though he were frowning. Douglas stroked his bird's head.

"Humans tend to assume eagles are fierce, I suppose because we view the bird as forever frowning." He smiled. "These look-like-they're-frowning brows are actually the eagle's sunshades." He chuckled. "When Sandose sees me in sunglasses, I wonder if he thinks I'm frowning." The eagle moved its head in quick starts, surveying items of interest. Douglas looked with the eagle and asked, "See anything out there, Sandose?" Aside to me, he volunteered, "Sandose's eyes are four times sharper than ours. He even has zoom lens magnification." I was reminded of a study hall teacher in school we called Eagle Eye.

Douglas held his bird aloft. Sandose spread his wings, showing a wing airfoil that was a marvel of curved grace, from inboard leading edges to wing tips. "Beautiful," I breathed, and asked, "What's his span?"

"Six feet two." He lowered the eagle, kneeled, and rested his arm on his knee.

"What's he weigh?"

"I keep him at 6¾ pounds—good hunting weight." He paused, and went on. "A female in the wild would weigh around 8½, and span 6'8" to 7'3"." Sandose nibbled through Douglas's hair. Douglas smiled. "He thinks he's grooming lice." The eagle nibbled on. "When eagles feed, a few ticks and lice transfer to the birds. Since they can't reach head and neck lice, they must have a grooming partner." He chuckled. "I'm being recruited." He turned his head to give Sandose new areas. "If they don't have a grooming partner, multiplying lice and ticks will put the bird down, and out." He looked me in the eye. "They become so weak, they'd soon starve." He stood. "I control Sandose's head and neck parasites with flea powder."

I nodded and came back to a question bothering me. "Why has nature designed female eagles so much larger than the males?"

"I don't know. But she's not as good a hunter—too bulky. Not as maneuverable as the male."

I thought on that and decided the question should be, why is the male smaller? The answer is that smaller is more powerful in the air. His size would make him the logical hunter and territory defender. But that the female is so much larger left my curiosity in suspension.

Sandose lifted his tail and muted a white streak across the cement. Douglas studied the mute and announced, "He's healthy." He took a morsel of meat from a leather pouch on his belt and fed it to the bird. Sandose gulped it, spread his wings, and tugged at his jesses. I felt for the captive eagle. Douglas stroked his bird's head. "Want to hunt, Sandose?"

No, Douglas, I silently thought, the eagle wants his freedom. And thanks for bringing him to release. The falconer looked at me.

"I'd like to cast him one last time. Do you have time, Dan?"

Time wasn't a problem. The problem was, did I want to participate in falconry? The eagle raised its wings into flying position, and halfheartedly flapped. Of course, I thought, it's possible the eagle could escape during a hunt. I nodded yes.

"Shall we go in your car or mine?" As soon as he asked, he looked at the mute, smiled, and said, "Mine. If you don't mind, would you drive?"

Douglas sat in back, holding and talking to Sandose. Going up the switchback, I told him about the pair of eagles I saw hunting yesterday, and I asked how far back from the rim he thought we should travel to avoid their territory. He explained, "From a Montana sheep country study, we learned a pair of golden eagles claims about ten square miles."

That meant we should hunt at least two miles back from the rim. "How do they mark their claim in thin air?"

"Don't know. Interesting question."

Another question, about sheep and eagles, draped itself into my curiosity, for future asking.

Three miles from the rim, Douglas suggested I turn from the trail and drive across prairie until we jumped a rabbit. He chuckled. "To carry Sandose on my arm through a mile or so of bush kicking is too much." He paused and added, "European kings used to cast hunting eagles from horseback, on saddles equipped with an armrest." Suddenly a cottontail raced from dry grass at the base of a mesquite just ahead of us. I stopped, and we watched the rabbit. Quietly, Douglas talked to Sandose. A hundred yards away, the cottontail slowed, stopped, and crept into the mesquite. Quietly, we left the car. With Douglas leading, whispering in reassuring tones to his bird, we walked toward the bush.

When the rabbit scampered out, Douglas cast Sandose. With the eagle's leg bells tinkling and jesses trailing, the bird gathered speed and quickly drew within range of the running rabbit. I noticed the bird seemed to aim slightly right of the cottontail, as if hoping to force the rabbit to veer left. The eagle closed to striking range, still keeping slightly right. Then, in that split second before the moment of truth, the bird banked left. The rabbit veered left, directly into the radius of the eagle's already established line of flight. The catch for Sandose was simple, and I marveled at the eagle's tactics.

When we approached the eagle on the prairie with his kicking, squirming rabbit, the bird mantled, hiding his catch. I looked to Douglas. "What's to keep him from taking off now and escaping?"

"Eagles won't take off with an animal that's kicking and squirming." Douglas smiled. "Too unsettling."

The way the eagle struggled for balance, I guessed the cottontail was jerking in the bird's talons. After a moment, the bird became still, and I presumed the rabbit was dead, probably punctured like a sieve. Sandose ducked his head under his wing, as if to check his catch. Douglas eased near and kneeled beside the bird. Suddenly, the rabbit spasmed, and Sandose squeezed again. After the rabbit was quiet another moment, Sandose again ducked his head.

Douglas took a piece of meat from his pouch. Talking softly, he used the meat to arrest the eagle's attention, at the same time slipping his gloved and gauntleted hand under the bird. Expertly, he fed Sandose the morsel, simultaneously securing the eagle's jesses, forcing the bird's talons from the rabbit and onto his glove. Smiling, he stood and handed me the cottontail.

Secretly, I admired Douglas's skill with the eagle, and even though I wished the bird had escaped, I had to admit, falconry was intriguing. I took the rabbit and was surprised. There were no marks on the rodent's body. No talon holes, no blood, no gore. The rabbit was simply soft and limp. I looked at Douglas. "How come no talon punctures?"

He laughed. "Eagles don't kill by puncturing." He held the bird for me to see. "Look how dull his talons are." They were dull, and I chided myself for not noticing before.

"In the wild, they're even duller, from landing on sandstone cliffs, walking on the ground, and so on."

I thought I then knew how eagles made their kill, but wanted to give Douglas his chance, so I asked, "How, then?"

He held up his free hand. "By squeezing. By constriction. An eagle can't kill anything its talons won't encircle." He looked at his hand. "Golden eagle claws are about the size of a woman's hand for the female, smaller for the tiercel."

Remembering yesterday's jackrabbit, I raised my hand. "Wait a minute. Yesterday, I saw one of our wild eagles make a fist of its talons, and jab at a jackrabbit's head. If the rabbit hadn't zagged when it did, that eagle would have knocked him silly, wouldn't he?"

He smiled. "The eagle can only stun a jackrabbit by jabbing. The bird must then quickly circle back, grab, and squeeze."

The question my curiosity was holding about sheep and eagles let go. "How do eagles kill sheep?"

Douglas half-smiled. "I don't want to shock you, Dan, but I think that eagles killing sheep is a myth." He paused and added,

"I think lambs, even brand new ones, are too large for an eagle to squeeze to death."

He surprised me. "Then what's the eagle-lamb flap all about?"

"Try tax write-off." He shifted the bird's weight, and tentatively stepped toward his car, some distance away. I joined his step, and he continued. "If a rancher claims in his tax statement he lost umpteen lambs to eagles, does the tax man come out and make a carcass count?"

I half-smiled.

He turned to me. "Would you like to do an eagle-lamb experiment?" He glanced at his eagle. "With Sandose?"

His question surprised, and I had no immediate answer.

"Far as I know, it's never been done."

As we walked a few more steps, I thought on his proposition.

"Make an interesting feature for your wildlife program."

I shook my head. "The phone would ring the walls down." Nevertheless, Douglas's idea struck me as worth pondering.

"You could simply report it, then. If we came up with proof an eagle can't kill a lamb, that would do a lot for the eagle."

Of course, he was correct. I drew a breath. All right. Provided you can get a lamb that is absolutely the smallest likely to survive birth. We don't want to be accused of rigging."

Douglas smiled. "I know a farm where I can get just that kind of lamb."

III

Back at headquarters, Douglas placed Sandose inside the hen house while we wired fencing across the top of the chicken lot. We also fixed a four-foot-long perch in one corner. Finished, we agreed the lot was a good halfway house for Sandose and a suitable area for a lamb-eagle test. We were about to bring the eagle out, when I noticed our resident tiercel cruising just above the north rim, flying as if he knew where he was going. Douglas pointed ahead of the bird. "Another eagle. Coming down the rim. Half a mile."

I hurried for my binoculars.

About a quarter-mile upcanyon, the eagle faced into the gorge, and hovered, as if waiting for the oncoming bird. The new eagle sailed on toward him, sashaying along as if it knew where it was going. The tiercel rose to an altitude of a couple of hundred feet and continued hovering. The new eagle came on, flying about fifty feet above the rim. The tiercel watched the new eagle approach. When it drew near, he folded his wings and plummeted like a fighter bomber at the new bird. The strange eagle, a female, turned away, out over the canyon. The tiercel matched the bird's turn and plunged on, as though intending to ram the female out of the sky. The new eagle flapped away, heading back upcanyon. The tiercel checked his dive and zoomed up in a turning spiral that repositioned him above the canyon. The new eagle ceased flapping, angled back to the rim, turned into the wind, full spanned, and began climbing in circles. Immediately, the tiercel matched her climbing wheels.

Spiral upon spiral, the birds rose into the Texas sky. At what I guessed was about three thousand feet, the new female shortened her wingspan, pulled in her neck, accelerated to forty or fifty, and tracked straight toward the tiercel. The tiercel scribed an arc in the sky that put him several yards behind and to one side of the newcomer. The tiercel then pulled slightly above the stranger. With the "intruder" leading, the formation tracked arrow straight, paralleling the rim, aiming downcanyon. I had an inspiration as to what was happening.

"I presume there is a high altitude corridor in the eagle world, complete with escort, available to passing eagles."

"Seems logical. The tiercel probably understands that if an outside eagle penetrates territory at low level, the outsider could grab a rabbit on the way through." He laughed. "I'd like to see this stranger grab from that altitude, with that escort pressing."

I chuckled. "Who said 'dumb animals'?"

"Not me."

The eagles sped on, covering distance at a clip I thought should leave vapor trails. The tiercel tightened his gap on the intruder. "He's not giving the stranger a chance even to look at one of his rabbits. Wherever she's heading, that female's trip is obviously going to be nonstop."

At about the point above the canyon where I had seen the neighboring pair of eagles rise yesterday, they rose again. When they were as high as the speeding formation, they orbited, as if waiting. As the duo approached the waiting pair, the tiercel broke off his escort and began a wide circle. The strange eagle continued boring ahead. The neighboring pair formed a new, diamond formation with the single eagle. The three sped on down canyon.

"Pretty slick," I said. "The traveler has been handed off to downcanyon control." I lowered my glasses, and looked at Douglas. "How 'bout that?"

"Never seen such before—or know anyone who has." He looked around the canyon. "You've got an eagle gold mine here."

I nodded, and with the question of how eagles mark a territory still nagging, I helped bring Sandose from the chicken house. Inside the chicken lot, Douglas gently coaxed the eagle from his fist to the log perch. The eagle eyed his surroundings and seemed to settle his attention on the rim of the cliff behind us. Douglas slowly removed his gauntlet, sighed, and said to Sandose, "I guess we've hunted our last time, old buddy." He turned to me. "Shall I leave my gauntlet and glove? He'll probably come to your fist for a few days."

Why not, I thought. Although I didn't want to be a falconer, I wouldn't mind pretending a day or two. I smiled. "Sure." He handed the equipment to me.

"Slip them on. I'll show you how to handle him."

I put the glove on, then slipped the gauntlet on. The sheepskin covered most of my forearm. Douglas gave me a piece of meat, and directed me to lure the eagle to my fist. I lured, and Sandose flew to me. When he landed on my fist, the huge bird's wings brushed my cheek. While I fed the eagle the bite of meat, Douglas quickly threaded Sandoses' jesses in that special way through my gloved fingers. As Douglas worked, he warned, "Secure his jesses quickly, before he can grab places you don't want him to grab."

I nodded. Having the bird so near my face made me uneasy. His brown shoulder was no more than inches from my own, and his hooked beak seemed even less from my eyes.

"Don't worry about his beak, Dan," Douglas chuckled. "It's not a weapon, unless he's biting at what his feet hold." He raised his bare finger to Sandose's beak. The eagle opened his beak, looking threatening, but made no move to bite. Douglas moved his finger nearer. Sandose hissed, and opened wider, but moved his head back. "He'd fall off your fist backwards before he'd bite my finger." Douglas moved his hand to the eagle's talons. "Here's what gives his beak leverage. If he gripped my finger in these talons, he could tear it from my hand."

I decided I would never allow the eagle to talon one of my fingers.

Douglas then touched the bird's tail fan. "Have you noticed the narrow white band in Sandose's tail feathers?"

I nodded.

"Your wild eagles don't have it, right?"

I felt a little sheepish for not noticing. "Hadn't noticed."

"This band gives you the age of an immature bird. The first year, the white is wide, nearly the length of the tail feather. With second-year moult, it becomes narrower. Third year, narrower still, until at about five years, the white is gone and an irregular touch of tan may show. That's a sign the eagle has reached breeding age—maturity. Sandose is four and a half—almost, but not quite mature."

"Is the white band the same for male and female?"

"Sure is."

Sandose was getting heavy. I walked to the log, touched his talons to it, and relaxed my grip on his jesses. The eagle stepped to his perch, jingling his bells again. "Why the bells, Douglas?"

"If he escaped during a hunt, the bells would warn game of his approach. In a day or two, hunger would force him back to me for food."

I thought, "How cruel," and suggested, "Shall we remove them?"

Douglas swallowed, took the gauntlet, coaxed Sandose onto his fist, worked the bells from the eagle's ankle, and set the bird back. Saying nothing, he slipped the bells into his pocket. At that moment, I felt sorry for Douglas. He half turned to me.

"If you'd like, you can give Sandose his rabbit."

Within ten minutes, the eagle had eaten all of the rabbit, except for a small piece of intestine and hind feet. I was curious about the fur the bird ate. Douglas explained that acted as a swab to clean the eagle's crop, which, I might add, now bulged as if he had a tennis ball under its breast feathers. He further explained that tomorrow, the bird would cast a dry, sanitary pellet about 2 inches long by ¾ of an inch in diameter.

"The pellet will be fur, a few bones, and some twigs and rocks that stuck to the rabbit's flesh."

"How often should I feed him?"

"He'll eat a 2½ pound cottontail, or half a jackrabbit, about every thirty-six hours." Douglas smiled. "To and from town, you should find enough road kill rabbits to keep him." His smile widened. "You'll get strange looks from passing drivers, but you get used to it."

I chuckled. "Worth it. By the way, what's my legal problem, in case a Texas Parks and Wildlife type drops by?"

"My permit allows me to leave the eagle temporarily in another's care. If there's a problem, have them call." We were quiet a moment, and he turned to Sandose. "See you in a day or two." Quickly, he turned and left the chicken lot. His walk toward his car reminded me of a mother leaving her first child at its first day in school. Over his shoulder, he said, "Don't forget his flea powder. It's here next to the garage door."

That afternoon, Sandose drew the attention of our resident eagles. He was buzzed frequently, and once, I found the resident tiercel sitting on the ground near Sandose's perch. It was then I imagined the kind of reception Sandose was going to receive the day he flies free. I filmed the buzz scenes for a future program. Sunday night, before bedtime, I checked him again. He was perched on one foot, with the other drawn up into his breast feathers, apparently sleeping. Quietly I retreated back to the house.

Monday afternoon, I cut a small piece of raw steak, gathered my glove and gauntlet, and went forth to play falconer. Sandose flew straight to my fist. Awkwardly, I gathered and threaded his jesses through my fingers. Although I didn't have his feet pulled as snugly against my glove as I wanted, I fed him his reward. As soon as he ate, he seemed ready to return to his perch. I was glad and released his jesses. Off he went. I admit, to lure this huge eagle to me on command gave me a thrill. Yet, I felt it would be a greater thrill to see him returned to a free spirit; I was confident that would happen in a matter of time.

That evening, when I returned from my ten o'clock broadcast, I found a freshly killed cottontail on the road. Happy as a kid finding an Easter egg, I lifted the bloody mess from the pavement, placed it in my VW's front compartment, and continued toward the ranch.

Tuesday morning, I played falconer again. This time, Sandose seemed less eager to come to me. I took that as a good sign. Next day, he was definitely less interested. Then came Thursday.

It was Sandose's fifth day without bells and time for Douglas's daily training session. When I went to play falconer that Thursday, it was warm, and I wore a blue, short-sleeved knit shirt. Outside the chicken lot, I put on the glove and gauntlet, took the raw meat in my right fingers, and entered Sandose's world. On his perch, he seemed edgy. Thinking little of it, I offered my fist to the eagle. He balked. In soothing tones borrowed from Douglas's eagle vocabulary, I coaxed. The eagle remained on his perch. I waved the steak at him. He seemed interested, but not enough to stir him to fly. So, I placed the meat between my gloved thumb and forefinger. This was the first time I had done that. The eagle seemed more interested, but it still didn't fly. I talked again and shook the meat morsel at him. Sandose flew to my fist.

Pleased again at coaxing this eagle to land on my fist, I sought his jesses. His right foot covered that leather. In the second I spent deciding to try for his left foot, the eagle snatched the meat with his beak, gulped, and studied my blood-stained glove, as if expecting more. His jesses were still free. I was uneasy. Casually, he gripped my arm in his talons and hooked his beak into the stained leather covering my finger. I was startled. Gently, I shook my arm, and whispered, "No, Sandose." The instant my arm moved, the eagle clamped his talons on my wrist in a crushing vise grip: his death squeeze. Immediately, I knew I'd made a mistake and that, without his jesses secured, I was in trouble.

In the eagle's bone-crushing grip, my wrist stung. Sweat beaded my forehead, my mouth turned to cotton. Desperately hoping Sandose would leave me, I tilted my arm up. Instantly, his right foot shot down the gauntlet and his talons gripped my bare forearm near my elbow. The eagle's squeeze mashed into my flesh. I froze. After I stood a moment locked in rigid stillness, Sandose semirelaxed his grip, lowered his beak to the bloodstain, hooked into its seam, and ripped a gap, exposing my bare finger. I closed my hand tighter. Immediately, Sandose repeated his death squeeze on my arm and wrist.

IV

I'VE DONE DUMB THINGS IN MY LIFE, but playing falconer takes the prize. If I moved my arm, the eagle tried harder to "kill" it. If I held still, Sandose seemed to presume my arm was "dead" and it was time to eat. I felt helpless and stupid. Desperately, I wished for Douglas's leather pouch, full of meat. Momentarily, I considered using my free hand to push or knock the eagle from me. But that hand was ungloved, and fear of the bird's slashing talons at my face disquieted me. If I only had something to distract the eagle, I thought, and suddenly, an idea came.

With my free right hand, I took a white handkerchief from my hip pocket. I shook it once for Sandose to see and threw it across the chicken lot. Immediately, the eagle shoved from my arm, flapped, and pounced on the moving cloth. With equal immediacy, I scrambled through the chicken lot gate, latched it, leaned against the fence with my eyes closed, and shook. After a moment of recovery, I examined my arm. There were two red, indented spots on my forearm, above my elbow. The skin, however, was not broken. Thankful for the method eagles use to kill, I walked away. Sandose was on his perch, holding my handkerchief in his talons. I looked at him as I passed and said, "Sandose, our falconry days are over." From that minute, I turned my attention to the canyon's wild eagles.

To watch our resident pair, I needed a spot where I could see that part of the Palo Duro which seemed theirs. I hung my binoculars across my chest and hiked downcanyon. A mile and a half below my home, I paused and studied a hill I thought would fill the bill. The hill rose from the canyon floor on the south side of the stream. The rise was a juniper-studded, rocky mound, reaching about half as high as the canyon rim. On a pond in front of the hill, half a dozen mallards nervously paddled. The pond was perhaps a hundred yards long, and twenty or thirty wide. Cattails and willow sprouts edged the water. Several sprouts bore beaver tooth marks. I glanced down the pond. A dam of willow sprouts plugged the stream. My mind momentarily refused to accept beaver in the arid Texas panhandle. Regardless, the dam was there, holding the Prairie Dog Town Fork of the Red as if it were a cool mountain stream. For some reason, the ducks paddled with increased agitation, and then they abruptly flew, wings whistling. A hen flapped with an awkward beat and lagged. Suddenly, a falcon-type bird zoomed from out of nowhere, straight toward the hen. The falcon hit the duck. Duck feathers exploded into the air, and the two birds tumbled to the ground. I raised my binoculars. A peregrine clutched the duck.

As I climbed the hill, I reflected on the efficient ways of nature and how she had apparently programed the duck hawk to select the weak for dinner. I was reminded of the Finnish fisherman Lauri Rapala, who noticed that in a school of minnows, game fish invariably struck minnows with a flaw in their swimming rhythm. Believing he might be onto something, Mr. Rapala carved an artificial minnow with an artificial limp. The lure is astonishingly attractive to game fish, and soon Lauri Rapala had trouble meeting world demand for his discovery.

From the hill's top I had a panorama of the canyon for about two miles upstream, and five or six downstream. I dragged a log to the elevation's peak and arranged it so I could sit and wait. I didn't wait long.

At first I noticed only the male eagle, coming along about fifty feet above the rim. One of his legs dangled, as though he carried something. I raised my binoculars. The tiercel was carrying a

cottontail. In the edge of my glasses, the female appeared. The
two birds met, faced into the canyon, and rose. At three hundred
feet, the eagles edged close to each other. When their wings were
tip to tip, the birds rolled on their sides, toward each other.
Deftly, the female received the rabbit in her talons from the
tiercel's. Gracefully, the eagles righted. With the rabbit dangling
below her, the female set her wings and aimed across the canyon.
The set of her wings combined with the length of her dangling
leg and further dangling jackrabbit, gave her the silhouette of a
T. As she crossed the canyon, there was no doubt in my mind
about what her destination was. My question was, "I wonder
how many eaglets she has?"

When the eagle was almost across, I saw she was tracking for
the left side of the mouth of a finger canyon. She sank lower and
lower and lower. A couple of hundred yards from the draw, the
eagle's sink stopped, and her flight path gently arced upward. A
few yards in front of a gray rock jut on the draw's mouth, the
female backflapped, and landed in what looked like a high-rise
cave. I adjusted my glasses.

The eagle stood on a pile of sticks, built in the hollow of a
gray-walled rock cave. The cave was about 7 feet wide, and 2½
high. It appeared to face more into the draw than into the main
canyon. Weathered sticks protruded from the cave's mouth. The
hen eagle lowered her head, and dragged her rabbit inside.

I lowered my glasses and surveyed a route that would take me
where I could both see into the eagle aerie and build a photo
blind. To get where I wanted, I had to return home and drive
toward south rim. I passed the windmill and stable and followed
the gently rising trail to where it emerged on prairie, south of
the canyon. Here I turned left and headed for the draw holding
the eagle's nest.

Near the draw, I parked a distance from the rim. Quietly, I
eased to the canyon's edge. Looking across the draw, I found the
cave nest. I was too near, withdrew, walked upcanyon a quarter-

mile, and moved to the rim again. Satisfied, I searched for a place to breach the rimrock. A few yards away, I found a narrow notch. From tracks in the tiny natural cut, I discovered deer, coyote, raccoon, and aoudad sheep also used the access. I knelt to the notch, supported myself with hands on rock forming the incision's sides, and passed through the crevice. I emerged beside an upturning juniper, rooted below the rimrock. Using the juniper as a handhold, I maneuvered onto steep, loose erosion below the cliff. Traversing the slope toward the nest, I paused every few steps to check my line, making certain I advanced behind a tree or bush or ground rise. Slipping Indian style, I progressed nearer and nearer the aerie. When I was far down the slope, I stopped beside a thick-trunked, full-limbed cedar growing at an angle. There was no other adequate cover ahead. The nest appeared to be about a hundred yards distant. Through an opening in the tree's branches I raised my binoculars to the nest.

The hen eagle was settled on her aerie. The nest's platform of sticks was about six feet wide, four deep, and one thick. The jackrabbit lay to one side. She seemed contented, while I was impatient to discover how many chicks slept under her warmth. I checked my watch. Only forty minutes eagle watching time remained before I had to return home, and prepare to go to the studio for my six o'clock broadcast. Fifteen minutes later, the tiercel landed on the nest and cocked his head this way and that to his mate. Then he turned and flew. Flapping with apparent purpose, he crossed the canyon. I followed the male eagle with my binoculars.

At the rim, the eagle rose to about fifty feet. The tips of his primaries separated, curving up like graceful fingers. His head showed honey gold, and the inner half of each wing's front edge radiated golden. The tiercel maneuvered along the rim, to a point above a half-grown, round-topped cedar. After turning his head down at the bush, he sank toward it.

The eagle plopped into the cedar's willowy, limber top shoots.

Sinking into the bush, he thrashed like a duck walking in molasses. After thrashing a while, he spread his wings their fullest, and lay still, barely supported by top branches. The eagle then stretched his neck toward a sprig, opened his beak, clamped it on the sprig's stem, and snapped it. An eight- or ten-inch Christmas-tree-shaped sprig stuck out the side of his beak. Holding the sprig, he flopped out of the cedar with the grace of an overweight lady romping an amusement park airbag. Half-jumping, half-flying, the tiercel thrashed toward the rim. Suddenly his wings caught updraft air, and he was butterfly graceful again. He spread his wings maximum span, rose to canyon crossing altitude, swung his wrist panels back, and accelerated toward the nest. The eagle's head was thrust forward, with his mini-tree flowing along his neck.

Three or four hundred yards from the nest, the bird's altitude was considerably below the aerie. Fifty yards in front of the high cave, he arced up, slowed, backflapped, and touched down. The male eagle stowed his wings and stood statue still. A moment later, he stepped forward, bowed low to his mate, and placed the sprig in front of her. That done, he turned, and flew.

"Interesting," I whispered, and I impatiently waited to see what the mother eagle would make of the gallantly delivered sprig. On the spur of the moment, I named the tiercel Sir Galahad, because it seemed to fit. Idly, I wondered what purpose the sprig served in the eagle's lives. Whatever, the hen remained motionless, save for the blink of her eye. I paused to study the draw she made home.

The little canyon's sides were rocky and overgrown with juniper, which I presumed flourished on some lucky source of ground water lacking in other parts of the canyon. A tiny stream linked several clear pools glistening along the draw's sandy bottom. Erosion had widened the draw's solid rock mouth, forming a fifty-yard-wide V that yawned into the main canyon. Swallow-tailed butterflies fluttered near the stream. Birds, in-

cluding the colorful painted bunting, flitted, and from somewhere in the main canyon, a mocker sang its song.

I came back to the hen. She was still, so I turned to the problem of how I was going to convert the tree I was behind into a
photo blind. So near the nest, blind-building would have to be
a night project. I flagged my brain to check moonrise and moon-
set tables while I was at work.

At two thirty, I was about to leave, when two tiny white heads
wobbled from under the female eagle and pressed against her
breast feathers. The eaglets' heads were the size of golf balls.
Their eyes were black, and their beaks opened and closed. I
could hear their faint cheeping. One eaglet struggled mightily to
hold its head aloft and peeped weakly. The other eaglet's head
was steadier, and its cheep markedly lustier. The mother eagle
stretched her neck high and turned her head down to her
youngsters. The baby eaglets turned their heads up to her and
cheeped. She watched a few seconds, rose, and stepped to the
jackrabbit. The two eaglets lay in a love-grass–lined nest cup,
about the size of a cereal bowl. The stronger, and I presumed
older, eaglet scrambled on its belly toward its mother, flutter-
paddling its stubby wings. About halfway out of the nest cup,
the eaglet stopped. The younger hatchling struggled to follow,
with little progress. Both eaglets raised their heads and cheeped
without pause.

With her beak, the female eagle stripped fur from the rabbit's
chest. Her babies watched, heads wobbling. From time to time,
the eagle shook her head, flinging fur tufts into the air. Both
eaglets grew tired, and one at a time, they laid their heads down.
When the rabbit's chest was plucked clean, the mother eagle
hooked her beak into the rodent's rib cage and tore the chest
cavity open. She then probed her beak inside, extracted a small,
bloody morsel, and stepped to her chicks. The older eaglet raised
high, steady and sure. The younger eaglet's head swayed back and
forth. The older eaglet snapped the food from its mother's beak

and gulped. The littler eaglet grew tired, flopped its head back onto the nest, and cheeped. The hen eagle pulled a second bite from the rodent, and again leaned toward her chicks. The newest eaglet struggled to raise its head, fluttered to the nest cup's edge beside the older chick, and snapped the meat into its mouth.

The next seven bites were snatched and eaten by the older nestling, causing its crop to bulge. Apparently contented, the eaglet sank down into the nest cup and snuggled. The smaller eaglet was so tired, it could hardly hold its head up. The mother eagle leaned to the little bird with a fresh bite. The little eaglet swayed, snapped, missed, swayed, snapped again, and gulped the meat into its crop. The smaller bird then began cheeping again. The eagle tore a piece of liver from the rabbit and dangled the meat in front of her littlest baby. The older eaglet raised its head and watched.

The smaller bird snapped the meat, swallowed, and resumed cheeping. The older eaglet raised its head higher. The mother eagle tore another bite from the rodent and dangled it toward her little bird. The older eaglet stretched its head higher yet, blinked at its nestmate, and jabbed its hooked beak at the little bird's eye. The little chick screamed. A droplet of blood mushroomed from its lower eyelid.

The mother eagle offered another bite to her offspring. Both eaglets rose toward the meat. The older bird snatched this bite and held it in its beak, making no attempt to swallow. The littlest bird wavered and flopped its head back to the nest cup, as though unable to hold it up any longer. For a moment, the older bird continued to hold its head high, then it slowly snuggled back into the nestcup. Its beak still held the bite. With that, the mother eagle resettled over her brood, and the aerie was quiet once more. I was glad.

Driving across the prairie, I was unable to get the little eagle out of my head. I thought of all sorts of solutions to the smallest bird's plight, from nipping the older eagle's beak to taking the little eaglet out of the nest and raising it myself. In any case, it would have to wait for me until tomorrow.

At home, I showered, shaved, and dressed for television. As I was about to leave, my phone rang. It was Douglas. Without wasting time, he blurted, "Dan, I have a lamb. Don't feed San-dose. See you in the morning."

V

RIVING HOME FROM MY EVENING BROADCAST, I had second
thoughts about having a part in staging an eagle-lamb
situation. What could it accomplish, anyway? People who were
prone to believe eagles kill lambs will likely go on believing, regardless. And if the test became known, I'd forever be on the
SPCA's list. Not wanting to think about it, I turned on FM, and
presto, I was listening to a recording of myself predict morning
fog. "The magic of radio," I mused, and settled back. The moon
was bright, and the air damp and warm. But, I reminded myself,
panhandle Aprils can go from warm one day to a raging blizzard
the next. With that in mind, I decided to construct the eagle nest
watching blind before going to bed.

At the ranch, I changed clothes, gathered my red nylon back-
pack, and stuffed it with grubbing hoe, small shovel, pruning saw,
scissors, pliers, leftover chicken wire, and a couple of burlap feed
bags. It was almost midnight when I drove for the draw holding
our mother eagle.

At the juniper across from the nest, I paused and listened.
Gentle wind sighed the juniper's branches. Below, the stream
babbled, and from somewhere in the canyon, a bird warbled its
midnight serenade. "The magic of nature," I mused, and I slipped
out of my pack.

My first chore was to grub a notch in soil under the tree's
sloping base. Working quietly, I used dirt from the notch to
form a level floor under the tree. When the floor was about three

feet by four, I wired chicken wire under low-hanging branches above. Next, I tied the burlap to the chicken wire. Both wire and burlap came to ground level, forming a four-foot-high dome. From neighboring trees I cut branches and wove them into the parent cedar, further covering the burlap's topside. Inside the blind, I cut a horizontal slit in the burlap. The slit was at my camera level. With the small pruning shears, I manicured a six-inch tunnel through the tree's growth, straight toward the eagle's nest. Finished, I pushed my binoculars through the slit, focused on the moonlit aerie, breathed, "Perfect," and repacked my gear. Driving home, I again had second thoughts about tomorrow's proposed eagle-lamb experiment.

The morning was foggy but comfortably warm. I was finishing my dishes when Douglas drove up. I went to meet him. He lifted the lamb from his car and set the animal on the cement. The lamb's umbilical cord was still attached, and its skin hung in loose folds. Shaking my head, I said to myself, "True, this has got to be the stupidest thing you've let yourself into." The little animal bleated, wobbled across the cement to me, and nuzzled my knee, as if expecting to find the magic of nourishment.

Douglas spoke. "Its mother refused to nurse it. It's called a slunk. I got it for ten bucks." Breakfast rumbled in my stomach. I was ready to abandon the project when Douglas gathered the lamb and strode toward the chicken lot. I stood on the pad. Over his shoulder he said, "We're about to make history, Dan. Get your camera."

"Crap," I muttered. Reluctantly, I gathered camera equipment from my VW and followed.

Douglas fumbled with the chicken lot latch. "When did you last feed Sandose?"

"About a day and a half ago. A small cottontail."

Grayson went in. "He should be hungry, but not starved." He closed the gate behind him. "I've wanted to do this a long time but was afraid of what my neighbors in White Deer would have thought."

I swallowed, sure I was thinking exactly what Douglas feared his neighbors would have thought. He walked to the center of the lot and gently put the lamb on the ground. I raised my camera.

Sandose eyed the lamb. Douglas backed outside and relatched the gate. The lamb bleated. Sandose riveted his eyes on the animal and moved his head side to side in that curious belly dancer head motion peculiar to prey birds about to fly. Watching through my viewfinder, I swallowed again and asked, "What's the lamb weigh?"

"Seven pounds. Average at birth is eight."

My breakfast rumbled again.

The lamb trotted toward Sandose's perch. Instantly, the eagle flew away, to a far corner. Bleating, the lamb followed and nuzzled up to the eagle. Sandose half-scampered and half-flew to the other end of the lot. The lamb stood still, as though bewildered. In a moment, it returned to about the center of the lot, and stood, bleating. Again, Sandose fixed his eyes on the little animal, moved his head side to side, and made a tentative start toward the lamb, paused, opened his wings, jumped into the air, and with one claw, grabbed at the baby sheep's muzzle. The lamb bleated and shook its head. Sandose scampered away once more, this time back to his perch. From that distance he studied the lamb, without moving his head.

Douglas unlatched the gate and went inside. "Let's let our bird get hungrier and let him think about it a while." He gathered the lamb into his arms. Instantly I felt relieved. Walking away from the lot, Douglas turned to his eagle and said, "See you this afternoon, Sandose." His voice was cheerful.

For the moment, I scored it lambs one, eagles zero, and I hoped it remained so.

When we put the lamb in the garage, I told Douglas about

finding the resident eagle pair's nest. Looking surprised, he asked to see it. "Sure," I said, "I need to set up a camera anyway."

Douglas and I stood by the crevice breeching the rim. Fog hovered just above the rim. The canyon itself was hazy but fog free. I pointed the aerie out to Douglas. He looked at it through his binoculars, declared it, "Nice," and asked, "How many chicks?"

"Two."

"Interesting." The tone of his voice said he found it more than just interesting. In a moment, he shifted his glasses across the canyon, to north rim, and asked, "Where does the tiercel stand guard over his nest?"

I said I didn't know. For that matter, I didn't know the male even stood guard, although his question was logical. Douglas focused his glasses and announced, "Got him." He lowered his binoculars and pointed to a peaked yellow cliff across the way. "See that dot, twenty or so feet below the peak?"

I nodded and raised my binoculars. No sooner had I found the eagle than it launched. The bird flapped with determination, heading upcanyon. We looked ahead of the eagle's flight. In the distance, a white-headed, white-tailed American eagle was coming downcanyon, sailing just above the rim and just below the fog. Near that point where the tiercel seemed to make a territorial stand, the male eagle flapped toward the American. The newcomer angled away from the rim, toward midcanyon, and descended rapidly toward the stream. The tiercel raced toward the other bird. Nearing the stream, the American eagle turned over it, leveled five feet above the water, and flapped downstream. Frantically, the tiercel dove at the invader, buzzed over its head, shot past, banked left, quickly circled back, and settled into a slot slightly higher than, and slightly behind, the American eagle. The interloper reduced wing beat frequently and cruised on, holding five feet above the water. The tiercel continued to follow closely, matching the eagle flap for flap.

The low flying formation came on downstream and passed in front of us. Their flapping wings harped the air. On and on downstream the birds went, and in a moment, neared the imaginary line I estimated should be the tiercel's southeastern territory limit. Here, the neighboring pair of eagles flapped toward the approaching formation. Near that invisible line, the tiercel broke off, and circled. The American flew on. Immediately, the neighboring male eagle settled into the tiercel's vacant slot, and the new formation continued downstream. I lowered my binoculars. "Amazing. Eagles apparently have a foggy day corridor."

Douglas lowered his glasses. "And don't stop for a drink, or a rabbit." He chuckled again. "Have to admire the way the tiercel kept the other bird moving. Herded it right on through."

I nodded. "Wish I knew how that bird marked his territory line. I mean, suburbanites build fences, and coyotes have scent posts. Those a guy can see, but for an eagle, in thin air—"

"Let me know when you make the discovery." He said it as though sure I would. I wasn't that confident.

The tiercel returned to his post on the cliff. With the eagle world normal again, I led Douglas down the trail to my blind. Inside, I set up my camera then helped him cut another slit in the burlap and a tunnel to the nest. Just as we finished, the mother eagle quietly lifted herself from her chicks and flew across the canyon. Quickly, we made additional slits to enable us to follow her flight. As she approached the cliff, the tiercel also flew. Both birds then flew to the rim and landed, side by side. After sitting quietly a moment, they groomed themselves, including an exchange of head feather grooming. They sat another moment, and then, slowly, the hen eagle bowed and flattened her back. The tiercel opened his wings, and like a butterfly, lifted into the air. Deftly, he floated over the hen. The female eagle gathered her tail fan to one side, and the male gently settled on her back. For fifteen or twenty seconds, the eagles copulated, manipulating their wings in the wind for balance. Finished, the tiercel lifted back into the air and resettled beside his mate. The hen eagle roused and shook her feathers.

Douglas smiled. "His reward."

I considered their act more romantic: a reenforcement of their pairbond, a strengthening of their relationship, a confirmation of their love, if you will.

In a few minutes, the mother eagle returned to the aerie. The tiercel continued sitting on the rim. When she landed on the nest, the littlest eaglet awoke, raised its head high, and cheeped. Without hesitation, the mother eagle began feeding her youngster. I began taking pictures, and after the third bite, the older eaglet awoke, scrambled toward its mother, and snatched the next eight bites. Stuffed, the bigger eaglet settled back into the nest cup, laid its head down but kept its eyes open, watching. The hen fed the littlest bird two bites. As the eaglet took another piece of meat from its mother, the older bird raised its head, eyed the chick, and struck at the back of its head. The older eaglet clamped its beak on the matchling's white down, twisted back and forth, and pulled a tuft out by its roots. The little chick screamed, turned, stretched its head as high as it could, and struck back. The chick's beak hit a stick next to the larger eaglet's wing. Immediately, the older bird jabbed the little bird again and twisted another tuft away. The chick screamed and fluttered out of the nest cup. The older bird watched the hatchling scramble over the nest's rough sticks and head toward the back of the cave. About halfway back, the little bird stopped. The older eaglet lowered its head to the nest cup's edge and fixed its eyes on the chick.

Douglas turned to me. "That's known as the Cain-Abel battle." The hen came to the nest cup, and resettled over the older bird.

I was almost afraid to ask, but I had to know. "How does it turn out?"

"Depends." The littlest eaglet fluttered back and disappeared under its mother's warmth. "If the oldest, Cain, is a tiercel, and the youngest a female, there is a chance she might grow rapidly enough to equalize the fight." He shrugged. "Time will tell."

"And if?"

"*If* it's the other way 'round, the little bird, Abel, will probably be dead within two days." He frowned. "Not so much from injury as having been starved out."

"Then why don't we take it from the nest?"

He frowned again. "First, its illegal."

"Only if caught," I blurted.

Douglas thought and said, "It would take four months feeding and caring for, Dan." He took a breath. "With Uncle Sam breathing at me, I can't help."

"If I'm caught, what's the penalty?"

"Five grand." He then added, "For molesting, transporting, or possessing . . . including any part thereof. Feathers, claws, and so on."

I looked toward the nest. "Sure a waste of eagles." At that moment, I knew I was going to do something about the Abel's plight. I didn't know what, but something.

Douglas raised his binoculars to the aerie. After studying it, he lowered them. "If I were you, I would say nothing about this nest on the air, or to anyone."

"How so?"

"Some people hate eagles so much, they would travel miles to destroy eagles in this canyon."

I remembered some of my schoolmates' eagle reaction in Ruidoso, and I understood. Douglas looked at his watch. "Shall we see if Sandose has an improved appetite?"

I was surprised. "So soon?"

"I think he's hungry enough. He just needs to think and to gather courage. Maybe he's done that."

I nodded, and we left. Climbing to the rim, I noticed our fog seemed to be thinning.

On the way home, I told of the green branch I had seen the

tiercel bring to the nest, and I asked its significance. Douglas said he'd heard about that, but no one had yet come up with a logical explanation. I resolved to find one.

Almost as soon as Douglas stepped from the chicken lot, Sandose set himself and flew onto the lamb's back. The lamb collapsed into the dirt. Instantly, the eagle bound its talons to the animal's rib cage and squeezed. I cringed and closely watched the lamb's breathing. The bird's talons reached only little more than halfway around. Still, remembering the crush of their vise grips, I worried. Although its breathing was labored, the lamb was breathing. With my own breath, I unconsciously tried to help the little animal.

At twenty minutes, Sandose left the lamb, waddled to the fence, and looked across the prairie, as if tired, or searching for easier prey. The lamb got up, tired but much alive, and bleated. Douglas and I cheered, and he remarked, "If Sandose weren't caged, he'd leave this minute and hunt something easier." In a moment, however, the eagle left the fence and again jumped up on the lamb's back, shoved it to the ground, and again bound talons to its chest cavity.

For forty-seven minutes, the eagle tried to stop the lamb's breathing, but was unsuccessful. Douglas was overjoyed at his bird's failure and grew more so as time passed. At forty-eight minutes, the eagle, apparently frustrated, began tearing at the lamb's wool skin with its hooked beak. Apprehension washed over me. Douglas noted that never before had he seen an eagle tear at the skin of a live animal. His observation didn't make me feel any easier about it. For several minutes, however, the lamb's skin proved too tough for the eagle. Then, at an hour and seventeen minutes, Sandose discovered a patch of tender skin under the live lamb's foreleg. Here the the eagle drew blood. My heart sank.

VI

DOUGLAS RESCUED THE LAMB, and we carried it to the house. In my kitchen we put A & D ointment on the lamb's small wound. Even though Sandose finally drew blood, I was happy with the outcome. "In the wild," I chortled, "a wrestling match that long would attract the whole countryside. Ranchers, tourists, television crews." I laughed. "There'd be time enough to build bleachers and to sell tickets."

Douglas smiled. "If we didn't sell tickets, every coyote within miles would bound in and steal the eagle's catch anyway." He became thoughtful and said, "We've made history."

I thought so too and was satisfied that in nature, an eagle was not likely to attack a lamb. My reasoning was based on that moment when Sandose left the lamb and went to the fence. There's little doubt in my head, had the eagle been free, he would have flown. Thinking ahead, I worked on how to gracefully handle our experiment on my weekend show. Skeptics would shout questions, I was sure, and some might take potshots. Instantly, one question loomed. I felt sheepish for not thinking of it before allowing my elation full sway. I looked at Douglas. "Could the larger female eagle kill a lamb?"

He waved his hand, as though brushing my question aside. "The average lamb at birth is a pound heavier than our little slunk. Also, consider how much stronger a lamb would be that had nursed at least once." He paused and added, "And there would be the mother sheep to contend with, too." He raised his hands.

My mind relaxed and I asked the logical, "Then how did the myth that eagles kill lambs get started?"

He smiled and settled back in a way that said I was in for a speech. "I believe that myth may have originated in the days of European feudal lords and serfs. Many lords were probably kind and generous with their vassals. But a few probably weren't." Douglas shifted. "Let's say a mistreated serf is watching his mean master's sheep. On a lonely mountain, miles from the lord's castle. One evening, after the master had been unusually unkind, the serf is suddenly hungry. For lamb chops. Next day, when the master comes to count his sheep, the serf simply points to the sky and tells about this giant eagle that swooped down and grabbed a lamb." Douglas pointed skyward. " 'Carried it right up into the sky, master.' " He shrugged. "Who's to dispute the serf's word?"

I smiled. "Today's sheepmen?"

"As I said, that myth makes them money. I think they work to keep the myth alive."

"What about stories of ranchers who say they have seen eagles feeding on dead lambs?"

"I would guess a coyote or bobcat or dog killed and opened the lamb, and the eagle came later to feed on what was left."

"Stories about eagles carrying a lamb high into the sky, and dropping them to death?"

Douglas looked at me as if to ask, "Are you crazy?" I shrugged. "If I'm to do an eagle-lamb program, these questions will follow —I need all the answers."

He nodded. "An eagle's motor is its breast muscles." He made a fist and held it up. "A little more than this—I doubt if the bird could taxi from the ramp with a lamb."

"How much can an eagle carry?"

"With perfect wind and sloping terrain, about 3¾ pounds. Two and a half pounds would be about a normal top load."

"Pictures I've seen of a dead lamb laying in a nest, in front of drooling baby eagles?"

"Salted into the nest by a camera-owning rancher with a skeptical tax agent." He frowned. "Of course, an eagle could carry a scrap of lamb picked up from a carcass on the prairie."

I shifted. "Why couldn't an eagle make a fist of its talons and knock a lamb silly in the head?"

Douglas nearly laughed. "If an eagle hit a lamb like that, the first time would be the bird's last." He took a breath, almost impatient. "I know what you're getting at. But remember, a lamb wouldn't be running with the speed of a jackrabbit. That, coupled with the lamb's higher weight, would shatter an eagle's hip sockets if he fisted a lamb." He shifted. "Eagle legs are not made for walking. Therefore, the bird's hip sockets are particularly weak. Bopping a lamb just wouldn't work for an eagle."

"Stories of eagles carrying away small children?"

"You'll think I'm crazy on this one."

I shifted. "Try me."

"You've heard how primitive Indian mothers gave birth?"

"Sketches."

"When her time came, she went alone into the wild. Sometimes, especially if the baby were a girl, she left it to die, because girls weren't valued as much as boys."

I nodded. "Those newborns were called *woodscolts,* right?"

"Right. But when the mother returned empty-handed, there must have been times when elders showed disappointment. The mother may have then pointed to the sky and explained, 'A great eagle carried my child away.' " He shrugged. "Fireside stories, I think, have kept that myth alive."

For the moment, at least, I had no more questions, and we became quiet. At last Douglas observed, "Some skeptics will die hard."

"Their problem." I thought and added, "To the real diehards, I'll suggest they bring their checkbooks and their eagle. We'll see how much sense a little wager will work into them." Outside, the sun broke through, flooding the kitchen with new light.

Douglas laughed. "You wouldn't."

"Heck I wouldn't."

"I'd like to be here for that." He became pensive. "But I'll be gone in seven days." He slapped the table. "Hey. We haven't fed Sandose."

I went to the refrigerator and removed a clear plastic bag containing a road-killed cottontail. Douglas took the rabbit from the bag. We stepped outside, heading back to the chicken lot. As we walked, I wondered why myths die hard. Is reality so illusive that we cling to myth for comfort? For example, take the myth that snakes won't crawl over a rope. I know that isn't true because I once tested it and filmed it, with a five-foot diamondback and an old lariat. Yet, some people responded to my film with disbelief or disappointment. The most common fault mentioned was the rope I used wasn't horsehair and that I'd find sure enough snakes won't crawl over horsehair rope. Personally, I think snakes make no effort to classify rope. Yet, if I were a cowboy, sleeping under the stars, I'm sure I would loop my lasso on the prairie around me, and I would crawl into my bedroll believing the myth too, because I would desperately want to cling to it. So here Douglas and I were, shaking the roots of an eagle myth some people will just as desperately want to believe. But that's all right. I don't have time to crusade. At least in my mind, I have separated fact from fable, and that's what is important for me.

Nearing the chicken lot gate, Douglas slowed, stopped and looked at the eagle. Sandose riveted his eyes on the rabbit and moved his head side to side. At last Douglas nodded. "I'm ready to release him."

I felt both happy and sad. Without another word, Douglas

opened the gate and placed the rabbit on the ground outside. Sandose immediately came to the gate, waddled out, pounced on the rabbit, and proceeded to "kill" it. The eagle squeezed the rabbit's rib cage for what seemed an instinctive time length, almost as though the time period was preprogrammed in the tiercel's brain. Finally, the bird relaxed its talons, and with the rabbit in one foot, hooked its beak into the animal's rib cage.

As the bird fed, Douglas whispered, "If you'll get scissors, we'll notch his tail feathers so you can keep up with him."

I went to the house and returned with scissors. Douglas pointed to the resident tiercel, circling high above. We exchanged smiles.

When Sandose was nearly finished eating, Douglas slipped his hand under the eagle and grasped its ankles. Holding the complaining, flapping eagle upside down, he took an aluminum band and pliers from his pocket, and I helped attach the numbered band to the bird's right ankle. We then clipped a one-inch notch in the middle of the eagle's tail fan, and Douglas set his bird back on the ground. Sandose seemed to glare at us, shook his feathers out, and returned to the rabbit. Above, the resident tiercel continued circling.

After Sandose finished eating, it was a while before he realized he was free. When that fact hit him, he simply spread his wings and flapped away, heading south. Instantly, the circling tiercel dove on Sandose. The resident male eagle relentlessly pursued the freed eagle, pressing until they both flapped up and over south rim, out of sight. At that moment, Douglas whispered, "Goodbye, Sandose. And good luck."

When Douglas was ready to leave, I admitted that I had known of him before we met and had foolishly allowed my disapproval of keeping a bird captive for falconry to prejudice my feelings of him as a person. Now, I admitted, I was glad to have met a falconer: that he had taught me not only about eagles, but had improved me as a person.

He smiled and said, "No sweat." I appreciated his generosity, and he went on to tell me the importance of my writing up our eagle-lamb experiment, and of submitting it to the scientific literature. I assured him I would, and he loaded the lamb back into his car for return to the rancher and to bottle feeding with other slunks. Warmly, I shook his hand and wished him well in the military. He said he'd try to come back to the ranch once more before leaving, but if he couldn't make it, he'd come back on his first leave. He also asked if I'd keep notes on Sandose's life in the wild and on how the two hatchlings fared. I promised to do the best I could, and he started his car. When he drove away, I was saddened.

The rest of the day I spent writing up our experiment, and then I went to do my early broadcast.

Next morning, I drove to the blind right after breakfast. The day was a warm, perfect spring one. When I arrived at the blind, the mother eagle was brooding her family. Her posture was as regal as a queen's, and I thought of her as Her Majesty. At 9:30, I filmed the tiercel as he landed on the nest with the bloody front half of a limp jackrabbit. Hardly pausing, he grasped the remains of yesterday's rabbit and flew away with it. Half across the canyon, he dropped his cargo of refuse. "Some lucky group of ants will find the eagle's gift and stock up for the winter," I mused, with reinforced appreciation of nature's way. A few minutes after he left, the tiercel returned, carrying a green cedar sprig in his beak. Gallantly, he bowed to his mate and placed the sprig in front of her. "Sir Galahad," I whispered. Advancing my camera film, I again wondered, "What for?"

At 10:05, the mother eagle fed her youngsters. The littlest eaglet got more meat than before, but it still seemed to get the short end of it. After the eaglets were fed, the mother eagle began feeding herself. Before she had taken her second hunk of jackrabbit, Cain began raining a torrent of jabbing unrelenting hammer blows at the little chick. Jab after jab raked Abel's eyes, head, and back. The tiny eaglet screamed, fluttered its wings, and paddled its feet. The older eaglet paused, eyed the chick, reared, and jabbed again, twisting a hunk of down from the hatchling's back. Abel screamed and frantically fluttered up over the nest cup's edge. Cain jabbed the retreating bird's back. For the first time, I noticed a dime-sized, watery sore, glistening on the chick's back. I swallowed.

Abel struggled on its stomach across the nest, again heading toward the back of the aerie. The larger eaglet stopped at the cup's edge, propped itself tall with its stubby wings, and watched the little bird. At that point, I had a possible clue about the Cain-Abel battle.

At the back of the nest, the little eaglet lay down, breathing hard. The older bird lowered its head to the edge of the nest-cup and continued to watch. I thought it significant the older bird didn't pursue beyond the nest cup.

After five or six minutes, Abel raised its head, wriggled around, and struggled back toward the nest cup. Immediately, Cain propped itself high with its stubby wings on the nest cup rim. The little bird lowered its head back to the nest's sticks. The two birds looked at each other, and after a while, the older bird slowly lowered its head again. Half a minute later, Abel inched forward. Instantly, Cain raised his head and glowered. The littlest eaglet seemed to glower back, drew itself up, and fluttered on, toward the nest cup. The bigger hatchling waited. When Abel neared, Cain struck at the younger eagle's head. The little chick dodged, and the big eaglet buried its beak in the nest. Abel scrambled on. Quickly, Cain raised his head and struck again, jabbing the little chick's raw back sore. Hurriedly, Abel passed Cain and stumbled down into the nest cup. Cain turned and jabbed the small nestling's head, twisting more down away. Suddenly, Abel raised his head and jabbed back, striking Cain's shoulder. The older bird lunged and twisted a hunk of flesh from the small one's back. Abel screamed. Blood rose from the wound. Struggling, Abel struck at Cain again and twisted a beakful of down from the bigger bird's shoulder. The older bird jabbed again into the chick's back, again twisted flesh away, jabbed, and twisted once more. Abel screeched and flattened against the nest cup's bottom. Cain jabbed at an eye, raking its hooked beak across the soft pocket above the eyelid. A line of blood formed. Abel lay motionless. Cain maneuvered into a favorable position and hammered a series of savage blows to the chick's head, back, and eyes. The little eaglet screamed and flinched and fluttered and tried to crawl under the larger bird. Cain increased the tempo of its attack. Abruptly, Abel turned and scrambled out of the nest cup. Cain clambered out behind and struck an especially hard blow to Abel's head. Weakly, the small eaglet crawled away, toward the back of the cave. As before, Cain stopped and watched. This action doubled my confidence in my growing theory behind the cause of the battle.

Next to the wall, the baby eaglet lay still. A fly landed on its back wound, followed by a second. Behind me, a noise sounded. I turned. Douglas was coming into the blind. Two climbing ropes were draped over his shoulders and across his chest. I smiled, and helped him inside.

VII

ALTHOUGH I WAS GLAD TO SEE DOUGLAS with his ropes, at the same time I was troubled by the thought of separating the littlest eaglet from its mother. In the back of my mind, I had what I hoped might be an alternative solution to the problem of the Cain-Abel battle. I turned to Douglas. "I've noticed that as long as the little eaglet stays out of the nest cup, the bigger eaglet leaves it alone."

Douglas's expression invited me to continue.

"The first-hatched eaglet may already be a territorial creature. Since it was there first, it may feel that the cup is his."

Douglas raised his binoculars to the nest.

"Either way, if one of us went into the nest, and filed the sharp point off Cain's beak hook, maybe Abel could gain enough strength to hold its own, and maybe the battle would stalemate."

He lowered his binoculars. "Worth a try." He smiled. "Who's going into the nest?"

"Flip you for it." I took a quarter from my pocket, flipped it, and put it on the back of my hand. "Heads you go. Tails, I go."

He nodded.

I uncovered the coin. "Tails."

Looking disappointed, Douglas brought a tube of ointment from his pocket and handed it to me. "May as well doctor while you're there."

Appreciating his foresight, I smiled and took the tube. From another pocket, he produced a small postage scale. "May as well weigh 'em, too."

Again I smiled. One question, however, bothered me. "What about the parent eagles. They may claw my eyes out."

Douglas shook his head. "For some reason, the parents don't claw our eyes out when we bother their aerie."

Strange, I thought. "Why?"

He explained that until modern man, with modern ropes, the eagle had never known a threat to their lofty nest. It is Douglas's feeling that since for millions of years, the eagle has not needed to develop a nest defense, they are at a loss to know what to do now. "Give them another hundred years of modern man's intrusion, and the birds will probably come at us as readily as a mocker or jay. But for now, they seem baffled."

Baffled suited me. With that, we left the blind and rigged ropes. Half an hour later, I backed over the rim, and rappelled down to the eagle's aerie. Across the canyon, Her Majesty and Sir Galahad circled. I was relieved to see them so far from the nest. Abel's back was a wet, raw sore. Additionally, its right eye was battered shut. Both eaglets lay still, watching through black eyes with tiny, midnight blue centers. I treated the smallest bird's wounds then lifted it to the scales. The little bird screeched. Its body was warm and soft, and I was surprised at the thickness of the eaglet's down. It tipped the scales at six ounces. Cain weighed thirteen. Next, I sliced meat from the rabbit and offered it to Abel. Eagerly, the little bird snapped the meat, plus seven more bites. With a fatherly feeling, I placed the eaglet back in the nest cup and lifted Cain, who complained and struggled. I then took my nail file and trimmed the needle point from the bird's beak hook. Finished, I patted the two, told Cain to be kind, and rappelled down the cliff. Once I was on the canyon floor, Douglas pulled his lines up from topside. Feeling better about the little eaglet, I started walking out of the canyon, heading for a sign of the game trail I knew would lead me back to the rim. In the distance, the two eagles continued circling.

It was past noon when I arrived back at the blind. Douglas said the mother bird came back and resettled over her chicks a few minutes after we cleared her nest. Sir Galahad was perched at his guard post. We settled down to wait for Her Majesty to leave. While waiting, I gave Douglas the eaglet's weights and told of feeding the youngest. He explained that was an advantageous feeding, since it only takes four ounces of rabbit to make one ounce of eaglet. "Calves," he added, "require nine pounds of feed to make one pound of beef."

At 1:30, the hen eagle fed her chicks. Abel seemed stronger and was able to get nearly its fair share. Silently, I took at least some credit for its new success. When Her Majesty finished the feeding, she flew across the canyon and landed beside her mate. Almost as soon as she left, the older eaglet attacked the little one. Although Abel was driven from the nest cup, as near as we could tell, it suffered no damage.

Douglas smiled, and said, "We may have done it." Silently, I hoped so.

At 1:45, the tiercel suddenly flew, heading across the canyon, rowing his wings with determination. Both Douglas and I raised our glasses to the eagle. When the bird was more than halfway across, I glimpsed the wing beat of another bird ahead. I adjusted focus. The other bird was a horned owl, flying as though unaware of Sir Galahad's apparent chase.

Douglas leaned forward. "What's a horned owl doing out at this hour?" He fine focused.

"Search me."

Ahead of the owl lay a mini-forest of tall cedar trees growing from the mouth of a finger canyon. A few trees reached forty feet. Sir Galahad flapped his maximum, gradually closing the distance between him and the owl. Douglas volunteered, "Owls and eagles aren't on good terms. In fact, owls relish eaglets." He chuckled again. "This should be interesting."

Suddenly the owl flapped at a panic rate. The two birds sped ahead, and when the eagle had gained to within fifty yards of the owl, the night hunter frantically flapped into the finger canyon's mouth. In a flurry of feathers, the owl turned toward a tall cedar, and disappeared into the middle of the tree's thick cover. Sir G. flew to the cedar and orbited the tree several times. Finally, he headed back to his perch and Her Majesty.

At 2:00 it was time for me to leave for work. As we left the blind, I felt much better about the little eaglet. At the rim, we paused. All was quiet in the eagle world. We stepped on, toward our cars. Abruptly, Douglas stopped next to a harvester anthill and pointed. One of the red ants was trying to take a mesquite bean seed into the hill's opening. The ant was having trouble getting the large, irregularly shaped seed through the hill's passageway. After unsuccessfully trying different angles, the little insect hoisted the seed with his front legs. Looking like a miniature front end loader, the ant carried the seed ten or eleven inches across the ground to a fist-sized stone. Here, the ant pressed the seed against the rock and rubbed it back and forth.

I kneeled. "I'll be darned. That ant is sanding rough edges from the seed."

After sanding the seed, the ant carried it back to the hill's entrance, tried again, failed, and again carried his load back to the rock. After more sanding, the ant tried again. This time, the insect squeezed the seed through the opening, and disappeared into the colony's underground granary.

Douglas turned to me. "Better write this up too. Title it 'Harvester Ant Uses Tool.'"

I rose, and we walked on. "Your turn."

He shook his head. "Tomorrow, it's Uncle Sam and me."

"I'll write it in your name."

"Why not both our names?"

I shrugged. "Minor."

At our cars, Douglas looked south and idly wondered, "Wonder where Sandose is."

"Haven't seen that little rascal." I chuckled. "Probably has a girl friend somewhere downcanyon."

Douglas smiled and got into his car. "See you on my first leave."

I saluted, and he drove away. Watching, I nodded and mused, "Nice person."

In the next two days, the Cain-Abel battle continued, but without damage to Abel. Again, I smiled. Three more days saw the little eaglet's sore healed, with new down covering the old wound. At about this same time, the bird's increasing size and activity blended the nest cup into the nest's sticks and out of existence. With the nest cup gone, the Cain-Abel battle ended. That reinforced my theory that the battle may be territorial. What would result, I wondered, if next year, I went into Her Majesty's nest at the battle's first sign, and erased the nest cup myself. Also at this time, I noted Sir Galahad stopped bringing the green cedar bough to the nest. That led me to believe the bough had served as a fence, to keep the little birds from tumbling over the nest's lip. Now that the eaglets were larger, the male bird must understand they had developed eyesight and sense enough to recognize the danger themselves. If that were the case, it was a good thing. Sir Galahad was so busy bringing food to his youngsters and defending his territory, he would have been hard pressed to bring the bough too. Also at this time, Her Majesty spent less and less time on the nest during the day. However, she continued brooding her eaglets at night. And I was surprised at how rapidly the hooked point of the older eaglet's beak grew back.

The Saturday morning after Douglas left, I awoke to snow. As weatherman, I had predicted sunny and warm. "Probably an inverted trough," I muttered, irritated at the knack I seem to have for not catching inverted troughs before they fall on me. My phone rang. It was a good-humored female viewer, saying she just swept an inch of sunshine from her walk. We laughed together, and I silently took solace from the fact inverted troughs are usually short-lived.

After breakfast, I drove for town, intending to catch up on errands and shopping which had been put off since my eagle involvement. The switchback was tolerable, however, I suspected when I returned, I would likely be forced to park on top and walk down. I shrugged, reminding myself my definition of a weatherman is a guy with fifty thousand dollars worth of scientific equipment and a hunch.

It was nearing dark when I was coming home. About a mile from Currie Ranch's north gate, I drove into a curtain of dark, writhing clouds. Wind rocked my VW, and from nowhere, a tumbleweed raced across the road, nearly hitting me. I watched the bounding weed as it spermed the earth with next years tumbleweeds. Suddenly, I was surrounded by fast-falling, wet snow. I turned on the war's windshield wipers.

Near the gate, the road became slick. At the same time, something flickered in an odd way from the fence, beyond the gate. I felt forced to give my attention to driving, yet the flickering continued to interrupt me, like a small child on the lap of a father trying to read the evening paper. Momentarily, the wind skidded my car. I did some corrective steering. Persistent as a damp day fly, the floundering on the fence continued to demand my attention. I slowed for the gate and carefully turned in. The flopping on the fence looked like a dead eagle. My spine crawled.

VIII

Rusty wire held the eagle by its wings. Its golden head hung limp. Pink fluid dripped from its nostrils and blew away in the snowy wind. Blood caked the bird's breast, and wind bent the eagle's wing tips into graceful curves. Its legs dangled. I swallowed, hoping against hope the dead eagle was not Sir Galahad.

I searched the snow for tracks. There were boot prints, nearly obliterated by my own. I untwisted the wires. The bird was almost stiff. Carefully, I laid the eagle in my car's front compartment, and with a heavy heart, drove on for home.

I tend to be a thinker, and as I drove into the snow, I tried to imagine why anyone would kill an eagle and then advertise the killing by hanging the bird on a more or less public fence. After sorting it out, I concluded the killer probably has a manhood problem. Maybe hanging the eagle for public viewing is supposed to be proof of his machismo. "There are better ways," I whispered.

The snow increased. I switched the VW's wipers to high and mopped the glass. A dark spot remained. Impatiently, I remopped the spot. The blemish floated, as if detached from gravity. Squinting, I scrutinized the particle. The spot was an eagle, low over the road, flapping toward me. My first thought was, "Her Majesty?"

As the eagle approached, it altered course, adjusting passage on my left. A feather was missing from the bird's right wing. My spine crawled, and I wondered, could it be the dead eagle was her mate and that Her Majesty is looking for him? Was it possible

63

for one eagle to miss another? "Nonsense," I muttered. At the same time, I couldn't ignore the question: Why then is she flying in this mess when she should be brooding her young? Her Majesty's misty image flapped abreast, fifty yards across the white prairie. Feeling strange about the mother eagle flying in the snowstorm, I stopped and watched, reminded of the time I saw buffalo rally 'round one of their kind in trouble.

During the great buffalo slaughter of the late 1800s, Charles Goodnight's wife withheld information from "hunters" about a small herd of the animals that had refuged in a canyon on their ranch. The hunters moved on, and in ensuing years that herd survived. Today its descendants live on the 30 x 20 mile JA Ranch southwest of Clarendon, Texas.

Buffalo are migratory, moving from winter to summer pastures with seasonal changes. One afternoon on the JA, I watched a herd of perhaps thirty animals munching its way south. Slowly they worked up to a fence that was blocking further progress. A large bull munched up to the fence. When he could no longer reach the grass he wanted on the other side, he set himself and pushed his chest against the fence. The top wire popped like a taut guitar string. Leisurely the bull stepped over the lower wires and munched ahead. Other buffalo followed, until a cow somehow caught her right hind leg in the fence's lower wires. Instantly the bull, and other buffalo, came to her. As the cow strained against the wires holding her, her fellow buffalo raised their tails and milled around her, brushing against her as if to offer reassurance. They continued this until she pulled free. I can't pretend to be a buffalo, but the animal's reaction to one of their kind in trouble touched me. Was their reaction an instinct to protect the trapped cow against predators that might have taken advantage of her situation? Or were the other buffalo acting from compassion?

*   *   *

Eye injury from Cain-Abel battle.

Raw sore on back of Cain-Abel battle victim.

Eagle-lamb experiment.

Dan True weighing eaglets and taking Cain-Abel battle victim from nest.

Golden eagle.

Author feeding eagle weakened by lice and ticks.

Note spoilers on top of wings.

Baby American eagle.

Eagle eggs.

1

Hatching eagle egg.

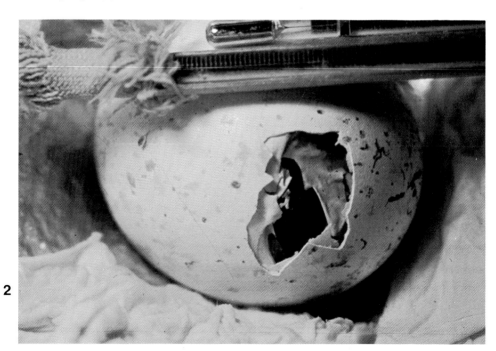

2

3

4

Eagle carrying cottontail.

Launching eagle.

Her Majesty disappeared into the snow. Uneasy, I drove on. A few minutes later, a dark line appeared through the snow ahead, marking the land's transition from prairie to canyon. Short of the cut through the rim, I stopped. The trail down glistened, slick and dangerous. "Crap," I muttered, and turned the VW's ignition off. I was dressed in Levi's, red wool shirt, and cowboy boots. From the backseat, I gathered a silver belly hat with stockman crease, and I snugged it tight. From the car's glove compartment I took deerskin gloves, pulled them on, turned my collar, and stepped out. Rapidly, I debated whether to take or leave the eagle. Deciding I should bury the bird, I tucked the eagle under my arm and strode off.

At home, I laid the eagle at the corner of the garage and hurried inside. From the woodbox, I gathered an armload of split cedar, and built a fire. The flames snapped and popped as it grew. I removed my gloves and held my hands to the blaze. Watching the flames, I fantasized how primitive ancestors must have felt when they returned from a hunt to their cave fires. Companionship with family and friends. Roasting meat from the day's stalk, telling tales of the adventure, stirring the fire, and retelling the hunt's high points. A fire burning exactly as this, from exactly this kind of wood. As I absorbed warmth, my thoughts returned to the eagles.

If the dead eagle is Sir Galahad, I was concerned at how difficult it would be for Her Majesty to provide for her growing family. I was also concerned over her ability to protect her territory alone against hawks, owls, and other eagles. And how would she cope with her head lice problem? Then I remembered a saying of my mother's: 95 percent of our worries never happen, so why worry? I nodded my head and whispered "Right." Anyway, maybe the dead eagle is a migrant, or maybe it was killed some distance away and brought here. I shrugged and laid plans to go to the nest as soon as possible. Then, toward the bunkhouse, I glimpsed motion. I turned, idly noting the snow had stopped. I saw nothing unusual. Even so, I was drawn to go outside and check.

Quietly I stepped the snow-covered walk beside the pool, toward the cement pad and the corner of the garage where I had placed the dead eagle. At the corner of the bunkhouse, I stopped and peeked around. Instantly, an eagle flapped away from the carcass. The eagle was Her Majesty. I stood still, and watched her fade into the canyon's deepening darkness. The gloom swallowed her. I stood another moment, then turned and slowly trudged back to my den and my seat before the fire. Gradually the fire burned itself into glowing coals. Suddenly I was tired. I rose, and went to bed, knowing I would get an early start at watching Her Majesty.

Morning came with only scattered clouds. Wind was light northerly, putting updraft air on south rim. I built a fire, and scanned the rim. For forty minutes there was nothing. Then, a speck above the rim. I lifted my binoculars. The speck was Her Majesty. A limp rabbit hung from her talons.

The eagle moved along the rim. At a point straightaway from the dead tiercel, she rose to about three hundred feet. For what seemed a long time, but was probably no more than five minutes, the eagle simply hung there in the air, moving neither right nor left, nor up or down. After a while, I had the feeling that Her Majesty could see me, that she was watching me where I stood in front of the window. I watched a few more minutes. The eagle made no move. Sheepishly, I drew the drapes and watched with my naked eye through the smallest possible slit. In a moment, Her Majesty moved, ever so slightly up, then minutely down, fractionally left, back right. After a long pause, she rose another hundred feet, shortened her wings, and headed toward the dead tiercel's location. I shoved the curtain apart. Instantly, the distant bird spanned her wings and turned away, back toward the canyon rim. I snapped the drapes shut, feeling guilty for having so tested the eagle's eyesight. After a moment, I cautiously squinted with one eye through a minimum rift. The female eagle was motionless above the rim. After a while, she finally shortened her wings, and once more headed toward the dead tiercel.

When Her Majesty landed with her rabbit next to the lifeless eagle, I knew she was a widow. But did she? After she had stood most of the afternoon beside her dead mate, I presumed not. Once, when a low-flying airplane passed, she mantled over her mate, shielding his body from view. As dusk settled across the canyon, she stepped away, occasionally pausing. Slowly, almost unwillingly, the widow turned into the wind, opened her wings, and launched. Flying low across the canyon floor, she looked back once. At the rim she rose, and steered downcanyon, I supposed to the duty of brooding her young for the night.

In front of the evening fire, I wondered if she would return in the morning. Next morning, when she didn't come back, I was sure she understood. It was then I decided to pick up each road-killed rabbit I found. I intended to place the rabbits where she could easily find them and to carry them to her young. However, I was worried over two other problems she was bound to face as a widow eagle: defense of her nest and territory; and the problem of blood-sucking head lice that were now free to increase.

In Sunday's noon sunshine, I walked up the switchback to get my car. At the rim, I scanned the canyon for sight of Her Majesty. Perhaps a mile and a quarter downcanyon, the widow was wheeling in blue sky high above the gorge's edge. She seemed to be searching the prairie below, and I guessed she was hunting. On her fifth turn, she suddenly set her wings and entered a medium-steep dive, coming my way. On line with her projected flight path, I brought my glasses to the prairie. Less than a quarter-mile from me, a nearly grown jackrabbit hopped under a mesquite. I returned to the eagle. She seemed to be slicing toward that mesquite. I imagined how wind was singing over her feathers and how land below her wings probably looked. As she approached the mesquite, the female eagle zoomed low, spread her wings, flapped more than necessary, and sailed directly over the rabbit. Her shadow crossed the rodent. At the same time, she slapped the bush's upper branches with her wing tip. Just past the bush, she turned into a sharp climbing turn, and looked back across the top of her wing. The rabbit crouched low under the bush. The eagle continued her turn, trimmed for landing, descended rapidly, and plopped on the ground a few feet from the mesquite. On the run, she half-hopped and half-flew at the bush. The jackrabbit bolted and scampered across the prairie. The eagle pushed back into the air and flapped after the running rabbit. The rabbit veered, into the wind. The eagle banked to match the rabbit's course change, straightened, and accelerated her wing beat.

By running directly into the wind, the rabbit created a speed advantage over the eagle. While the rabbit's ground speed was minutely reduced by the head wind, the eagle's ground speed was cut by the exact velocity of her head wind. The rabbit sprinted on, easily outdistancing the slowed eagle. From a safe distance, the rabbit hopped into the air as it ran, as though checking its margin of safety. Doggedly, the hen eagle flapped on, skimming just above the grass. As she watched the rabbit's image shrink, the eagle reduced her flap rate, as though she knew she was beaten. Gradually climbing, she slowed even more and angled back toward the rim. The rabbit slowed to hippety-hops. The eagle continued its course. The jackrabbit stopped, twitched its ears toward the eagle, and casually hopped under a larger mesquite. At the rim, the eagle rose and began a new series of wheels. Almost immediately, she stooped again, diving away from the rim.

Three hundred yards from the rim, Her Majesty roared through a covey of quail. All of the birds easily zipped away; she didn't come close to a feather of one. In fact, her tactic seemed more of a test than anything, a possible test to see if there may be one of the covey not feeling, or not flying, well enough to escape today. She pulled up from her stoop and banked toward the rim. Here, she rose and began a new series of wheels. I got into my car and drove for the road to Amarillo, hoping to find a road-killed rabbit.

I drove all the way to Amarillo. All I saw on the road were occasional flat patches of dried blood and cottontail fur. I returned a different route, via a stretch of Interstate 40 and then a dirt road called Whitaker Road that lead back to the ranch. Still no luck. Back at the gate, I decided I may as well return home, get my .410 shotgun, and hunt a rabbit for the widow eagle and her brood. As I drove across the prairie, the thought of her feeding a lead shot to her young caused me to change my mind from the shotgun to a .22 caliber rifle.

For three hours, I was no more successful at rabbit hunting than Her Majesty had been. Between kicking bushes on the prairies, I glanced at the sky and caught sight of her as she hunted. Once I watched her when she was about five thousand feet high, and probably a mile up-sun from the prairie dog town. She was apparently angling for an attack line to the village from out of the sun's disc. When she was where she wanted, she dove. Her dive was the fastest I'd seen, probably near her maximum of 175 miles per hour. When she had plummeted down to about fifteen hundred feet and half a mile from the town, she broke off, slowed, and turned back toward the rim. I guessed some sharp-eyed prairie dog lookout saw her and barked the alarm, and the town's population disappeared underground. I wished she understood how to hunt with me, as Sandose had with Douglas.

At the rim, she interrupted her hunting to challenge an intruding hawk. The hawk was well into her territory. Her Majesty dove on the hawk. The smaller bird easily outmaneuvered the female eagle and moved on. A little while later, I flushed a rabbit. It was a half-grown jack, and it exploded from the mesquite like a fuel dragster. The rabbit was easy for me to miss. Half an hour later, I flushed another. Although I came

closer, I missed again. A few minutes later, I jumped a cottontail and scored.

The sun was getting low when I placed the rabbit on a north
rim jut. From there, I drove across the canyon, to the parking
spot above my blind. Now the sun touched the Texas horizon.
Three minutes and it would disappear. Across the canyon, the
hen eagle rose. I raised my binoculars. She was carrying a cottontail. I smiled, until a red-tailed hawk floated into the side of my
binocular vision. The hawk headed toward the mother eagle. As
she rose, the hawk harassed her, as if trying to make her drop
our rabbit. Her Majesty could do little more than bat her over-
loaded wings at the hawk when it dove on her. When she reached
crossing altitude, a second hawk joined the first. The mother
eagle set her wings and started across. The hawks increased their
diving attacks. Not halfway, she suddenly dropped the rabbit,
shortened her wings, and flapped on a new diving course. The
hawks partially folded their wings and spiraled down after the
tumbling rabbit. I looked ahead of the hen eagle. A horned owl
flapped downcanyon, near to but away from her nest. I panned
back to the eagle. Her speed was high, perhaps 125. Closing
rapidly on the owl, she raced on.

From just behind the owl, Her Majesty extended her quarter
panels, checking her speed. Above the bird, she clenched her
feet into fists and jabbed. The owl's main wing bone snapped
with a crack. Instantly, the owl tumbled down in a thrashing
mass of feathers. The eagle pulled up into a climbing turn, as
though preparing to launch a sortie on the second owl. As she
dove toward the second night hunter, the owl flapped into a
cut in the rim which was heavily grown with short, plump
cedar. The eagle banked toward the cut. The owl hurried into
a thick cedar. Her Majesty buzzed the tree. As she passed over,
she positioned her primary feathers so that they would sing loud.
Past the bush, the hen eagle dropped rapidly toward the owl on the
canyon floor. On top of her wings, I noticed several rows of tiny

feathers pop up. The popped up feathers looked like *spoilers,* the devices jet and glider aircraft deploy to spoil airflow. The spoiled airflow causes loss of lift, which her rapid sink rate verified.

"How 'bout that," I whispered, wondering if aeronautical engineers had copied the eagle.

When the eagle approached the canyon floor, the owl floundered across the ground. Quickly, Her Majesty pounced and squeezed. As soon as the owl stopped quivering, she tore feathers from her prey's breast. That done, she severed the bird's wings, grasped its body in one foot, and launched, heading for her nest. I moved my binoculars to the aerie. There was no sign of the eaglets. I couldn't believe it. I sat down, nervously braced my arms on my knees, and fine focused. The nest was empty.

IX

I HAVEN'T DECIDED IF MY NEEDING ACTUAL PROOF before making judgment or turning a decision is fault or blessing. Either way, since I didn't see with my own eyes the owls molest the eaglets, I can only stumble along with heavy suspicion. Besides, I have found nothing in nature all bad. The horned owl is probably the single most deadly killer of rattlesnakes. Although I don't like the thought, I suppose an occasional eaglet is fair tradeoff. Regardless, seeing the aerie empty saddened.

With the owl in her talon, Her Majesty landed on the nest. She stood motionless a full minute, then she released the owl and tenatively stepped into her darkening cave aerie. She stood another moment, studying her vacant nest. As darkness fell, the mother eagle remained motionless. A few minutes later, I left the blind. Wondering where and how she would spend the night, I trudged back up to the rim and continued to my car.

The next few days, I discovered the widowed bird perched at night either on the yellow chalk cliff or on a gray rock cliff across the canyon. Her choice seemed to depend on winds. One morning, from my hill on the canyon floor, I spotted the lady eagle cruising the rim. Her crop bulged, causing her breast to protrude like a glider's half-hidden wheel. That satisfied me that she had just fed. The eagle sailed on a quarter-mile, dipped below the rim, and floated across the mouth of a small draw. Across the draw, she rose to the rim and sailed on. In a moment, she neared the high, peaked, yellow-faced cliff. Here she nosed slightly down, aimed for the cliff's face, arced up, spread her wings, backflapped, extended her feet, and landed atop the peak topping the cliff's face. The instant the eagle's feet touched the rock, her body pitched forward and her tail fan snapped up. At that moment, white underbody feathers flashed, giving the widow's thighs and legs a fluffed pantaloon look. Her body pitch reminded me of the rear view of a cancan dancer, flicking skirt and petticoats skyward. Quickly, the eagle recovered into her classical *a* pose and surveyed her domain.

After a moment, the widow roused and shook. With her beak, she collected oil from the special gland at the base of her tail. Then, working her beak through a primary wing feather, she oiled the feather, nibbling in a graceful arc through its tip. The feather flipped away, she collected more oil and dressed another. When her wing was finished, she preened a tail feather, from root to tip, and then two more. Pausing, she resurveyed the canyon. Apparently satisfied all was well, she roused and shook again. After sitting a moment, she stretched her neck high and preened breast feathers, working as far up under her chin as she could. She spent an unusually long time on all sides of her neck feathers, continuing to work up as high as she could. At last she roused and shook once more. After she resettled, the sun sparkled her eyes and cast an iridescent sheen over her plumage. She flicked her wings, alternately crossing and recrossing their tips across her rump. Apparently not satisfied with their set, she flicked and crossed them again. And again. Content at last, she sat looking regal as a queen, turning her head up and down the canyon. Then she lowered her head, raised her claw to it, and scratched, as a dog scratches behind an ear with a hind foot. Her scratching was awkward, mostly because claws are poor head scratchers. A few minutes later, she interrupted her scratching and launched, heading upcanyon with purpose. I looked ahead. Two hawks were coming downcanyon.

However hard the widow flew, the hawks easily outmaneuvered her lumbering attack. Next day, the hawks returned, flying as though they took glee in the eagle's inability to stop them. Over the next several days, the birds became regular invaders. Her Majesty seemed frustrated over her situation, and gradually she allowed the hawks to penetrate deeper and deeper into her grounds before she launched. At the same time, I noticed her attacks were increasingly halfhearted. Then, one afternoon, she simply sat on her peak and watched the hawks fly through her airspace. Her nonaction surprised me, and I wondered how long her new attitude would prevail. I frowned. Had Her Majesty given up her territory? Fifteen minutes after the hawks were gone, the widow eagle flew. Her flight said she had something on her mind.

The eagle aimed downcanyon. She crossed the gap of a finger canyon and sailed on. When she was far downcanyon, the neighboring tiercel rose, as if getting into position to defend his territory. The widow continued running the rim, remaining low, until she was near the higher tiercel. Here, she turned into the wind and hovered, facing into the canyon. The two birds hung motionless, suspended in the Texas blue like topaz-colored gems. In a little while, the tiercel slowly descended and eased toward the widow. When he rached her altitude, he poised a hundred yards off her wing. The widow drifted slowly toward him. I interpreted her maneuver as asking permission to enter his territory. Instantly, the tiercel rose. Just as instantly, the widow drifted back. The male eagle waited a moment and again descended to her level. After a moment, the female eagle gently dipped earthward. She dropped forty or fifty feet and rose back to her starting altitude. Her flight looked as though it could be eagle talk for "Hello there." Almost imperceptably, the tiercel drifted a few feet nearer. Instantly, the widow dipped again, lower than before, and rose again. The male bird came a few yards closer. Suddenly, a third eagle, a female, boldly sailed in near the tiercel. For a long moment, the three birds held steady. Then, slowly, the widow turned away and headed back upcanyon.

To me, it appeared our lady eagle had flirted with her neighbor.

"Why not," I mused. "One never knows how many eagles yesterday's guns took until one checks."

When Her Majesty had traveled about a mile, she began circling straight up, rather than continuing to drift along the rim. And up she went. In a few minutes, she was wheeling high above the canyon. Each time she swung into the sun, leading edges of her wings winked golden. Wheeling higher and higher, she was soon a speck against the sky. She paused between circuits, and I hoped she would quit right there. She didn't, and I whispered, "Keep climbing, ma'am, and you'll go out of the sight of my binoculars."

From my flying experience, I knew the air at Her Majesty's altitude was crisp and cold. My mind pictured how earth appeared from below her wings. The canyon would look like a thick-trunked, hollow tree. The gorge's side canyons would look like stubbby limbs from the trunk. The eagle's image stabilized, longer than before. Again, I hoped she was happy with her height. Then, slowly, she began another wheel. Half-around, going away, her image profiled blade thin. Briefly, she was invisible, then she reappeared in broader profile. Eyestrain speckles gave me problems, and my arms were tired. The bird was barely visible at the end of her circuit.

"Please, bird, not again," I whispered. The speck that was her held steady, a motionless atom in the atmosphere. Then, Her Majesty's minute image drifted into the beginning of another wheel. As she turned, I lost her again. Humorously, I guessed maybe she was going up to jump and end it all. Another side of me argued, that is hardly characteristic of a thirty-seven–million-year winner—maybe she's she just killing her fleas and lice, either through lack of oxygen or freezing. I half-smiled, waiting for her to reappear. The sky remained blank. Quickly, I calculated the bird's probable flight path. From there, I eased my binoculars through a corresponding track. Nothing. I moved on around her projected route and stopped where the eagle's circuit should end. The space remained blank. I shifted half a diameter higher; half a diameter left; full diameter right. Down. Left. Up. The sky was empty.

I sat quietly a long time and pondered the eagle's flight. In front of me, the stream babbled. A scrub jay occasionally squawked between the sweet song of the house finch. A single hawk moved easily along the rim, and an idea formed: maybe Her Majesty was announcing her availability to tiercels within eagle-seeing distance of her high flight. Aerial advertising? Seemed logical. Sandose? I wondered.

It was two days before I saw the widow again. I was atop my observation hill. The sun was warm, enhancing the scent of canyon juniper. A few yards away, a house finch sang a melody I first came to appreciate while recuperating from high fever in a thatched hut in Mulegé, Baja. At that time, I thought the little finch sang especially for me. Half a mile to my right, the eagle rose from somewhere unknown. Her leg dangled, as though she carried something. I fine focused. A small box turtle was clutched in her talons. At about two hundred feet above the rim she held motionless and dropped the tortoise. She watched the turtle fall, then closed her wings and dove. Down they went, tortoise tumbling, Her Majesty twisting and spiraling behind. At the last moment, she jabbed her leg at the turtle and clawed it out of the air. She spread her wings and zoomed her prize aloft. At two hundred feet she dropped and caught the turtle again. As she rose, a red-tailed hawk came down the rim. Her Majesty dropped the tortoise and fell in behind the hawk. I couldn't believe my eyes. Here was Her Majesty, flying along behind the hawk, almost as though she were lonesome and just wanted company. The hawk nervously kept glancing back at her. The two birds flapped in front of me and on upcanyon. I was surprised again when the eagle flew past the point I had never seen her go. I watched until she and the hawk went out of sight around a bend in the upper canyon. Half an hour later, she came back. Near the peak, she rose, retracted her wings into a *W*, and tracked across the canyon. Her flight was smooth, on a slight sink. Halfway across the canyon, she sank below the horizon, nearly blending with the canyon's background. Nearing the south wall, she leveled her flight path, then gently arced up, slowing as she neared the gray rock cliff. A few yards in front of her perch, she backflapped, reached her feet forward, and landed. She went through the routine of stowing her wings. That done, she drew one foot into her breast feathers and dozed. It was the first time I had seen her sleep in daytime. Somewhere I read tiredness is a sign of depression. I wondered if an eagle could experience that emotion. Or were her multiplying head lice sapping her strength. How do you catch an eagle for a flea powder dusting? I wondered.

Three days later, I was surprised to see the eagle laying on the gray rock shelf. This was the first time I had seen her laying down. I looked extra close. Her head was up, as though she were at least keeping an eye on her domain. Her head feathers were unkempt. In addition, I thought she looked lonely.

The shadow of an eagle-sized bird flashed my vision. Her Majesty cocked her head up, as if eyeing the shadow caster. I lowered my binoculars. A buzzard, the first I'd seen this spring, flew along the rim. Compared with an eagle, the vulture's flight was tipsy and less authoritative. In Mexico, the buzzard is called a *so-piloto,* or a so-so pilot. Even so, here it was, apparently just arrived from its wintering grounds near Mexico City. Remarkable, how birds migrate. The way they know exactly when to come and go. I've pondered the mystery behind their precise spring arrival and fall departure. Could it be possible migrating birds have a single-angle sextant built into their eyes, connecting to their brains? Such a sextant might respond to a specific angle of the sun and stimulate our feathered friends to point their beaks north or south and to flap. To compensate for cloudy days, nature could have designed the birds to measure the angle of ultraviolet rays. The buzzard moved on along the rim, its wings rocking as it flew. I refocused on Her Majesty. Her head was turned toward the vulture.

Behind me, a noise sounded. I turned. Douglas Grayson was climbing my observation hill. His right arm was in a cast and sling. He waved his arm aloft and smiled. "There was this big eagle—"

He couldn't finish for laughing, and I couldn't help laughing with him. I reached to help him up, tapped his cast, and asked, "Tax break?"

We laughed again, and he explained, "Freak accident on the Fort Bliss obstacle course." He scanned the canyon. "How are our eagles?"

"Eagle," I corrected. His expression said he caught my meaning. "We lost our tiercel and both hatchlings."

As I told him what had happened since he left, he took my binoculars and looked where I pointed. Douglas hardly had time to see Her Majesty before he said, "We'll have to catch her and dust her. Today."

I rubbed my chin. "How do you do that?"

He lowered my glasses. "By her ankles." He lifted his arm again. "I'll bury you in sand—along the stream." He turned and started down the hill. I followed. Talking over his shoulder, he went on, "I'll go to town and get a pigeon. We'll drive stakes on each side of your waist, tie a cord between them, and tie the pigeon in the middle of your stomach." He took a couple of steps. "When the eagle swoops down to grab the pigeon, all you have to do is grab her ankles." He turned, and smiled. "And hang on."

X

IN AN HOUR, Douglas was back with a pigeon in a small cage. From his car, he also took a sack, which I presumed held goodies one takes to the bush when capturing lice-ridden, female golden eagles. He glanced at me. "All we lack is a shovel and a couple of wooden stakes." I nodded and went to get them.

With Douglas leading, we shopped the stream for a suitable sandbar on which to bury me. It was obvious to me that where ever we chose, we would be forced to work within the eagle eye of Her Majesty. "After watching us, will she still come for our bait?" I asked.

"If she can count, we're in trouble."

"What do you mean, if she can count?"

"After you're buried, I'll leave. That's when we find out if eagles can count."

Half an hour later, I lay buried. Douglas placed a small log under my head. Next came a chicken-wire bucket we made from materials in his sack. The wire was garnished with cedar sprigs and had a small slit that gave me limited vision. I held the stakes as he drove them on each side of my waist. To the stakes, he laboriously attached a cord. With my help, he then tied the pigeon to the cord at a point over my sand-covered naval.

Suddenly, I was curious. "Where have you caught eagles this way before?"

With his cast, he pressed the pigeon against my stomach and arranged my arms along the sides of my body. As he fixed my gloved hands next to my thighs, he answered, "This is how Indians captured eagles."

His evasiveness discouraged me from pursuing it further. He scooped sand over my arms and hands and added a couple of scoops to my stomach. The pigeon squirmed. With his foot, Douglas worked the sack across the sand to him. Out came a green plastic bowl. He placed the bowl over the pigeon, settling the bird. Through a hole in the bowl's lip, he tied a black fishing line. Paying the line out, he moved off, and although I couldn't see him, I heard the crunch of his retreating footsteps in the sand.

"Douglas, I hate to mention it now, but I can't see much."

"You won't need to." His voice said he was only a few yards away. In a moment he was back, moving around me, dabbing sand here and smoothing the ground there. With a final touch, he stood. "Now, I'll hide in a cedar far up the bank. When I see her coming along the rim, I'll pull the bowl. Make sure the pigeon flaps and flutters." He paused. "After the widow grabs the bait, count ten. Study the position of her legs. Make absolutely certain you get both ankles at the same time. Otherwise, you're in big trouble." He took a breath. "Once you have her, hang on. I'll hurry." He paused again. "Any questions?"

"What if you're wrong about how much an eagle can carry?"

"Be nice, and she won't drop you from five thousand feet." Saying no more, Douglas walked from my vision.

When it was quiet, I appraised my situation. It didn't take me long to wonder how I had been talked into what now struck me as near idiocy. Indeed, buried in a sandbar, with a log pillow, a chicken-wire bonnet tricked out in cedar spray, and a pigeon trampling my naval. A moment later my body quivered from the sand's creeping cold and my nose itched. I twisted my mouth, but that did no good. I shook my head, and an incipient sneeze poised. I stopped breathing and closed my eyes. Slowly, the suspended sneeze subsided. I lay there, deciding that for sure, this wasn't something I would retell to casual friends. Then I realized it was possible Douglas had never caught an eagle by this method. When it was over, I figured I'd have earned at least the Distinguished Eagle Feather, with a Lice and Tick Cluster.

An airplane droned overhead. I was glad the pilot couldn't see me. The chill invaded deeper, and my eyes watered. Slowly, I closed them. I have never taken a tranquilizer, but now felt entitled . . . surprised in fact a dozen weren't included in Douglas's sack of eagle catching goodies.

After an hour, my body ached, the back of my head hurt, and my neck throbbed. Amused at my stupidity, I held my eyes closed, wishing I were in front of my fireplace sipping hot chocolate. Maybe this whole project was doomed to failure, I thought, because the eagle could count. I remembered reading that crows can count—that if two hunters enter a blind and only one leaves, the crows refuse to come near. I half-opened my eyes, and closed them again. The sun was a long way from down. Then, I thought I heard a distant whistle. I opened my eyes. The green bowl slipped from my stomach. The pigeon struggled, blasting sand in my face. I turned my head. My left eye held what felt like a canyon boulder. Tears clouded my vision and streamed down my cheek. I shook my head. The pigeon stopped thrashing. Quickly I looked at the bird. My eye throbbed. The bird was still, a blur, apparently bobbing its head. Suddenly, the pigeon beat its wings in frenzy, weaving, twisting, and pounding my stomach. Just as suddenly, the sky darkened in the slit of my vision. The rushing of wind split the air. An instant later, a brown overcast crashed onto my stomach. I gasped for air. At the same time, the eagle's huge brown body pulsated in front of my nose. I started counting. One. The pigeon struggled in the eagle's claw. Its head went in circles. Two. I blinked a tear away, and searched for the eagle's free foot. Three. I moved my head slightly, tracing Her Majesty's feathered leg to her ankle. Four. I blinked again. Five. The pigeon strained. Six. The eagle's free foot was on the sand beside my body, but outside of my hand, out of reach. Seven. Panic welled. The pigeon quivered. Eight. I realized my time was running out, and that if I didn't grab her soon, I might be forced to try again tomorrow. Another tear formed. I blinked it away, and suddenly the eagle yanked her foot up on my stomach and clutched the pigeon, squeezing the quivering bait with both feet. Her ankles were nearly together. Nine. Another tear welled. I blinked, silently commanded "Now!" and grabbed.

The eagle jerked its legs, beat its wings, violently grabbed my stomach with her talons, and screamed in a staccato, high-pitched voice.

"Hang on, Dan. I'm coming!" The legs of Doug's jeans joined the commotion. Burlap mixed with the eagle's beating wings, and abruptly the bird was less excited, jerking its legs with less frequency and diminished determination. Suddenly my chicken-wire bonnet popped off. I blinked against the sky's brightness. My lips and teeth were gritty. Douglas pressed a burlap sack to the eagle's head and smiled at me. "Hold her feet with one hand, and her wings with the other while I sack 'er."

I did as instructed. With his good hand, Douglas worked the bag over the eagle's head, past her shoulders and down over her body. He then slipped his hand over mine, and grasped her ankles. Grateful, I released my grip. "There's a leather thong in my pocket. Get it, and tie her ankles."

Slowly, I lifted my aching body from the sand. I pulled the thong from his pocket. I dropped my gloves on the ground, and with trembling fingers and bleary eyes, I tied the eagle's ankles in my best boy-scout square knot. Finished, I wiped my eyes. Douglas gathered the sack's opening and pulled it between the bird's feet. The sack lay still. The pigeon's limp body lay on the sand. Douglas beamed. "Works, doesn't it, Dan? And eagles can't count." He said it as though surprised at our success.

I stretched. Sand dribbled down my back. "It works." I brushed my jeans. "And lice or no, that creature has fizz."

Douglas came up with his sack, took a metal band from it and pliers from his pocket, and he kneeled to the eagle. Suddenly, he stopped. "This eagle is already banded."

I kneeled beside him. He was right. Rapidly, he fumbled the sack from between the eagle's feet and pushed it up. There was a V notch that also gapped the bird's tail feathers.

XI

AFTER DOUGLAS AND I STOPPED LAUGHING, we examined Sandose for lice. Douglas talked to the bird as we worked, telling him it was good to see him again, and asking how he was doing. Sandose's head lice population was almost out of hand. However, when we considered the possibility Sandose and Her Majesty might get together, we decided against dusting, on the grounds the female would ingest too much chemical. Smiling, Douglas gently talked to Sandose as he untied the eagle's ankles. Casually, he released the bird. The tiercel lay still a brief moment, seeming not sure it was free again. Then Sandose scrambled to his feet and leapt into the air. Flapping away, he raised his head and looked back over the top of his wing. As the bird mounted, Douglas waved and said, "See you around, little friend."

The eagle climbed rapidly toward the rim. It was then we saw the widow flying above the canyon's edge. At about a hundred feet, Her Majesty hovered, as though waiting. An eighth of a mile from the female, the tiercel reached the rim. There, he spread his wings and tail their maximum and rose. I found the notch in his feathers eye-catching. At an altitude equal to the hen's, the male eagle checked his climb. The two birds' heads moved as though they were inspecting each other.

Douglas chuckled. "She's probably making note of the fact Sandose is marginally mature. For breeding, that is." After a long moment, Her Majesty drifted toward Sandose.

"Maybe she's just measuring his flea picking ability," I suggested. The tiercel remained poised in position. When the widow was about fifty yards from Sandose, she paused, then slightly pulled her wings in and dipped. Again I felt she was saying "Hello there." However, Douglas said she was flirting.

After the female dropped fifty feet, she respread her wings and climbed to her original altitude. Sandose drifted a few feet toward her and stopped. Again, the female retracted her wings, dipped lower than before, spread her sails, and rose. After a long pause, the young man eagle eased a few yards closer. With more boldness, as though she were getting her act organized, Her Majesty folded her wings and nosed into a dive. Near the rim, she pulled out and arced skyward at an exhilarating angle. Sandose remained motionless, watching. With greater speed, the female repeated her folded-wing dive and climb. When she was stable again, she turned her head toward the male. After a short pause, the tiercel drifted nearer, narrowing the gap between them to twenty-five yards. The female closed her wings tight to her body and dove, sizzling like a bomb, below the rim. With wind tearing at her feathers, she half-opened her wings and rocketed up. At the top of her rise, she slowed, flipped into a wingover, and screamed earthward again. Sandose eased to within fifteen yards of her starting position and waited. Her Majesty zoomed up, slowed, and opened her wings. This time, she was only a few feet off the male's wing tip.

For a long moment, the two birds hung motionless, inspecting each other. Then, cautiously, the two eagles began semicircling, as though beginning a winged dance in the sky. Gradually, the bird's circles curved into sparkling pirouettes above the canyon. They didn't seem to notice as the wind drifted their aerial cotillion along the rim. Soon the female eagle waltzed like a deliriously happy brown butterfly. A mile downcanyon the birds flew together under an early rising moon. There, the eagles were met by the widow's neighbors. The neighboring eagles watched the two dance in the deepening blue sky for several minutes. Slowly then, Her Majesty led her dancing partner back upcanyon. Above the yellow cliff's peak, she circled twice. Sandose followed. Then she swung a wide, descending circle around toward the peak. On its pinnacle, she gracefully alighted. From several yards behind, the tiercel followed. At the peak, he hovered above her a moment and turned away. The widow's head twisted, following his flight. The male eagle completed a low circle, reapproached the peak, and poised in the air, a few feet above Her Majesty. Deftly, she sidestepped, as though offering landing room. The tiercel pulled his wings in, descended a few feet, lengthened his wings, rose, and circled again. This circle was higher and wider, as though he was not interested in landing.

After watching a moment, the female eagle spread her sails, lifted, and rose to the tiercel's altitude. The tiercel formed loosely on her flight pattern, and together they climbed, circling higher and higher, until at last the female leveled off. Again the eagles hung in the sky, at an altitude I estimated to be three thousand feet. The female looked at the tiercel, closed her wings, and plunged down. When she had dropped perhaps two hundred feet, Sandose closed his wings and followed. Her Majesty dove on, and when her speed was perhaps a hundred and fifty, she partially opened her wings and curved into a soaring climb. As her speed diminished, she turned her head and looked behind. Sandose was just off her tail, outside her wake, climbing with her. At the peak of her rise, she twisted into a wingover, and once again plummeted earthward. As the eagles passed, they looked at each other, and I was sure they exchanged throaty calls. The tiercel twisted and dove after the female. Her Majesty didn't seem tired anymore, and I imagined that her body quivered with excitement from the thrill of flight with Sandose.

After two more dives, climbs, and wingovers, the hen eagle again dropped to the peak. From the way she descended on half-open wings, without gaining forward speed, I was sure she had deployed her spoilers. Apparently she kept her spoilers operating right to the peak, enabling her to land without circling. Sandose descended behind her in an identical pattern, but at the last moment spanned and circled low. Coming around, his approach seemed less tentative than before. Without hesitating, Sandose landed six feet from Her Majesty.

With gusto, the female eagle began preening, rapidly working her beak through primary feathers. Sandose watched a moment and began preening his feathers, occasionally pausing to eye her, the canyon, the air above, and the female again. He acted to me as though he may be nervous, almost as if he expected a husband eagle to plummet out of the sky and tear feathers.

When Her Majesty finished her wing, she stood on one foot and scratched her head with a claw. Shortly, the tiercel also clawed his head. Occasionally the two birds paused and glanced each other. During a pause, the male sidestepped closer to the female. She resumed preening. He stood, watching. At last, Her Majesty paused. Sandose sidestepped next to her and slowly lowered his head. Douglas giggled.

Her Majesty spent a long time on the tiercel's head feathers. When she finished, she eyed the top, sides, and back of his head feathers, as if inspecting. Apparently satisfied, she bent her head to the tiercel. The male stretched and nibbled through her crown feathers, stopping now and then to flick a parasite from his beak and over the cliff. Her Majesty positioned her head at various angles, seeming to savor the feel of the male's beak scratching long-neglected spots. Suddenly, she leapt from the peak, flapping full force, aiming across the canyon. Sandose stood, watching after her as she flew away. Both Douglas and I turned our attention ahead of the female. In the gathering dusk, a lone horned owl flapped parallel to, and below south rim. The owl rapidly flapped into dark shadows of a tell cedar. Her Majesty turned and headed back across the canyon. New movement caught my eye along the rim. It was Sandose, flapping upcanyon away from Her Majesty. I pointed to the male eagle. Douglas shook his head.

"Dumb bird," he said. "He's leaving. Without even kissing her good night."

It was dark when Douglas and I returned to my home. Beside his car, he said he was sure Sandose would be back tomorrow. "He's that smart," he quipped, and he added, "I'll be back, too."

At sunrise, I was on my hill. The raucous call of a scrub jay chased by a mockingbird floated from the other side of the stream. A few minutes ago, a buck and doe had drunk from the pond and had moved downstream. An hour later, Her Majesty appeared above the rim to my right. She was coming upcanyon, alone, and since I hadn't found her on regular perches, I guessed she spent the night elsewhere. The widow approached the yellow peak and landed with that cancan-forward pitch. I smiled.

For half an hour the female eagle preened, rehooking vanes to barbs in feathers that needed it. When she finished, she sat still, except for her head turning slowly up and down the canyon. The rising sun warmed, and light south wind flowed across the gorge. The deer reappeared and redisappeared between cedar and mesquite, as they grazed their way downstream. A turkey now and then gobbled from somewhere, and the scrub jay continued screeching at the mockingbird. Her Majesty flew. I scanned ahead of her flight, upcanyon. About three miles distant, another eagle was in the sky, above the rim. The two birds flew toward each other.

The distant eagle was Sandose. Near that invisible line, he seemed to wait for Her Majesty. The widow flew on toward him, and in a few minutes the two were dipping and zooming through their "hello-how-are-you" ritual. Then the birds rose, at the same time coming back downcanyon. As far as I was concerned, it was good to see she invited him into her territory. Her Majesty descended to just above the rim. Sandose flew about a hundred feet above her and a little behind. I smiled.

Her Majesty flew parallel with the canyon's edge, sailing low from bush to bush, sometimes brushing her wings so near a bush top it looked as though she may have touched. The tiercel kept his hundred feet and followed. The eagles worked the rim, to a point directly across from me, and on, far downcanyon. Near that mysterious line, the neighboring eagles appeared. Without ceremony, Her Majesty steered back and circled behind the top of the canyon. The birds were out of sight a moment, briefly appeared, and disappeared again. They were hunting a new strip of land away from the rim. For a better view, I scrambled from the hill and worked my way up the canyon's rise behind me.

The eagles worked the strip back to their northwest line. Here, they circled up, soaring on board-straight wings, several hundred feet above the prairie. When Her Majesty was halfway around her first turn, Sandose followed her pattern, but in a track about an eighth of a mile away from hers. The birds' two tracks assured that between them, they covered every inch of ground below. A quarter-mile back from the rim, the bird's circles edged. With each wheel, they gained three hundred or so feet. At a circuit's completion, the tiercel paused and turned his head up and down the rim. A lone coyote trotted along the rim, sniffing at each bush as he passed.

"Bad day for the rabbits," I chuckled.

Sandose banked into another altitude-gaining wheel, offset a quarter-mile west of his first. The female tracked her assignment. Suddenly, she straightened her flight track, as though she may have spotted something. Immediately, the tiercel suspended his circuit and flew toward her. Simultaneously, the eagles backed their wings and dropped in a sweeping circle I guessed would set them on an approach to whatever quarry they appeared to have in their eyesight. With Her Majesty leading, they angled toward a solitary mesquite well back from the rim. Two hundred yards from the mesquite, the widow leveled, six feet over the prairie. A hundred feet above and behind, the tiercel leveled. Flying as though she were alive with excitement, Her Majesty glanced over her wing, as if to verify her new hunting partner's position. Then she angled up slightly and increased her altitude a few feet, as though checking the target. Fifty feet from the bush, she flapped with extra vigor. Suddenly, a young cottontail scampered from grass under the tree. Sandose dove, closed the distance, and grabbed. In a flurry of feathers and jittering rabbit, he stopped on the prairie. Her Majesty landed next to him. Instantly Sandose mantled over his catch, hiding the rodent from her view with his wings and tail fan.

XII

I WAS DISAPPOINTED that Sandose didn't share. After all, I reasoned, it was Her Majesty's rabbit. Surely he was bright enough to grasp that his hunting success was made easier with the female's bush beating help. Why didn't he understand the importance of sharing those benefits with her, I wondered. Could his sharing problem stem from his long hunting relationship with falconer Douglas? "Possible," I nodded, feeling more charitable. A few minutes later I spotted Douglas walking down the canyon toward my hill. I whistled, waved, and climbed down to join him.

On my log atop the hill, I told Douglas about the eagle's hunt. He frowned and said, "Although Sandose is close to maturity, the years he was with me may have robbed him of some natural learning. But I'll tell you this. Unless his manners improve, Her Majesty will send him packing when a mature male flaps by."

Her Majesty appeared alone above the rim. Slowly she rose and wheeled in hunting circles. Near the invisible line, she went into a shallow dive out across the prairie. Her stoop carried her below the rim, out of our sight. When she didn't reappear within a reasonable time, Douglas and I agreed she probably caught and was feeding. A few minutes later, Sandose showed up. His crop bulged. He rose and ambled off in the direction of Her Majesty's dive.

Sandose circled above the prairie where the female eagle should be. I chuckled. "Wonder what's she's thinking?"

Douglas laughed. "Whatever, his feathers should be burning." He shifted. "Could be worse. At least they're grooming each other. That'll keep 'em together a while—maybe long enough for him to smarten up." Sandose continued circling.

Behind us, a flock of robins chirped noisily. I turned to see what the commotion was. They were eating berries from juniper trees. Occasionally they flew to the stream for water and returned for more berries. Without turning around to see them, Douglas said, "Drunk, aren't they?"

He was right. The birds were getting tipsy from fermentation of the combination of fruited berries, water from the Prairie Dog Town Fork of the Red, and robin digestive juices. I nodded. "Yep. They're drunk."

Twenty minutes later, Sandose flew to the peak. A minute later, Her Majesty landed next to him. For the next half-hour, the eagles preened both themselves and each other so thoroughly I was sure neither had a single parasite left.

The day grew warm. Gracefully, the widow spread her wings and lifted. Sandose launched behind her, and the birds rose. At two or three hundred feet, the eagles aerial waltzed again. However, this time they seemed relaxed. After a few whirls, the birds climbed higher and began playing the high-speed game of dive-and-zoom-follow-the-leader. After several ups and downs, the female descended toward the rim. Sandose didn't follow.

Douglas observed, "I don't like that."

"How so?"

"I think he's about to be tested. For cooperation. To see if he'd make a suitable prospect for a mate."

"Sounds complicated. They're just birds."

"Strange thing about most prey birds. The female can't build the nest—has no idea about it. The male must do that for her." He paused. "No one has figured out why its that way. But it is, and he must understand that cooperation."

Her Majesty landed on the canyon's edge. The tiercel remained high, zooming and zipping on his own. The female clamped a tennis-ball–sized rock in her right talons and rose on the wind. Douglas spoke again. "For her to test Sandose, considering his stage of maturity, is an act of desperation. But, the moment of truth is at hand."

Sandose dove toward Her Majesty, shot past, arched up in front of her, slowed, spread his wings high in the air above her, and glanced down. The female carried her rock three hundred feet above the rim, turned into the canyon, and stabilized. The tiercel flipped into a wingover, dove, zoomed up, alternately folded and opened his wings, and dove once more. The hen eagle patiently watched. Her rock-holding leg dangled below. I heard one of the eagles chirp in a throaty voice.

"She talking to him?" I asked.

"No. He's the jabbering one—having a good time. She won't lead him on or give him clues. This trick he'll have to figure out on his own."

The male eagle retracted his wings, circled her direction in a wide, swinging descent, pulled up next to her, and checked his speed. He trimmed his wings to stabilize a few feet off her right wing tip. Douglas spoke. "Progress."

Both eagles' feathers glistened in the sun, and their eyes sparkled. The hen looked at Sandose. When she seemed sure she had his attention, Her Majesty opened her talons and dropped the rock. "Sandose, if you'd like to live in this part of the canyon, pay attention."

Sandose remained motionless. Her Majesty's rock tumbled down, hit the rim, and clattered into the canyon below. "Sandose, you're flunking," Douglas observed. Quickly, she deployed her spoilers and dropped. At the rim, she snatched a rock on the fly and rose to the tiercel again. Again, she dropped her rock. Again, the male watched her stone fall and clatter over the canyon's edge. "He may still be too young," Douglas breathed.

Slowly, the hen eagle rose, backed her wings, and aimed for the gray rock shelf across the canyon. Sandose watched her a moment, then zipped into a new series of aeronautical capers. At the top of a wingover, he chirped with apparent delight. I chuckled. "He's not a thinker, is he?"

"Right now, no more than a kid in a swimming pool on July Fourth."

For fifteen more minutes, Sandose cavorted in the sky, then he sailed across the canyon and landed beside the female. A moment after he settled, Her Majesty hurriedly flew and headed upcanyon. We looked ahead. Another golden eagle was leisurely coming down canyon. The widow furiously flapped toward the intruder. Sandose sat on the shelf.

The transient eagle avoided the widow's sweep and sailed on. The widow flapped after the newcomer, which was obviously another female. The new bird matched the widow's pursuit speed, easily staying ahead and coming on. Suddenly, the invader turned and flapped directly toward the gray cliff and Sandose. Douglas slapped his thigh. "This should be interesting."

Her Majesty turned after the new female, flailing a few yards closer to her. The intruder increased the tempo of her wing beat and flew on. In front of the tiercel, the stranger looked at Sandose and turned again. The widow eagle angled across the female's turn radius and closed the gap between them to within a yard. Sandose watched the two female eagles roar past, turning his head with them as they flew by. Both females continued flapping, gradually angling back toward north rim. Douglas chuckled again. "Will popularity spoil Sandose?"

In the distance, ahead of the two eagles, Her Majesty's south neighbors circled, waiting. The females flapped on. As they approached the invisible line, a line that was really beginning to bug me, the intruding female began rising. On the other side of the line, the neighboring tiercel matched her climb. Except for the widow, the two eagles rose higher and higher. The tiercel kept pressure on the transient female, not allowing her to enter his territory. I turned to Sandose. He seemed to be watching.

When the intruding eagle and the neighbor tiercel reached about three thousand feet, the female rigged for fast cruise and turned across the line. The tiercel assumed escort position, and the two tracked southeast. Douglas spoke. "Another reason why Sandose must understand cooperation."

"Wonder what Her Majesty said to him as they flew by."

"Nothing compared to what she's gonna say when she gets back. And here she comes."

Sandose had flown and was crossing the canyon toward her. One at a time, the tiercel and the female landed on the peak. The eagles sat until almost dark. Her Majesty was first to fly. She sailed straight to the gray rock ledge. Sandose followed, but not as close as before. The hen landed. The male approached, but aborted his landing at the last moment. Sandose circled a slow-turning orbit in front of her. Her Majesty flew, flapped through a circle beside Sandose, dropped out, and landed again. The tiercel completed the circle, reapproached the ledge, and again turned away at the last moment. The hen relaunched, accompanied the male eagle through another circle, and relanded. Sandose followed and landed six feet away from the she eagle. Twisting his head, he inspected air above them, and then up and down the canyon.

"Seems nervous," Douglas chuckled. "Like he's afraid a husband may come roaring out of the blue."

I nodded.

The female eagle pulled one foot into her breast feathers. Sandose settled down, and just before dark, he also pulled a foot into his breast feathers. Douglas sighed, as though relieved.

"Great," he said. "She's going to give him another chance."

XIII

NEXT DAY, HER MAJESTY did give Sandose another chance at her drop-the-rock game. Again, he didn't catch on. During the rest of the time Douglas was home, we didn't see her try again. Before he left, we were both struck by similarities between eagle and human life-styles.

Through the rest of summer, the bird's schedule changed little, except for hunting times. As the days became warmer, the eagles hunted early morning or late evening. The rest of the day they perched in the middle of cedar or cottonwood shaded by the south canyon wall. Considering a cottonwood exhales over a hundred gallons of cool water a day, the birds obviously appreciated natural air-conditioning.

Sandose continued hunting with the female, without sharing his catch. When scraps he left weren't enough, Her Majesty hunted again, alone. Since she put up with his behavior, I assume she was content to have his grooming and his company. At the same time, I hoped he was only going through a learning period, and that in time, he would graduate into adulthood. As to territory defense, the young male did no better. Since there were no eaglets to feed, I suppose that made little difference. Nevertheless, his lack of understanding there troubled me, and I guessed it troubled Her Majesty also. Then I wondered again, How was he to know there was a territory? Even if he were inclined to help her against invaders, how was he to know exactly where he was to draw the line? At the same time, I admired the female's patience, and I presumed she excused Sandose's shortcomings on grounds of immaturity. Then I remembered he was almost five. Wasn't it about time he caught on? I asked myself. My answer came one day in mid-December.

It was a sunny, windy morning. Nearing my observation hill, I noticed several teal feeding in the pool on the stream. I paused to watch. The ducks swam nervously. I moved nearer to them. The ducks rose, wing tips whistling. I turned toward my hill. From the corner of my eye, I noticed the water fowl circle for altitude. When I approached the hill, the ducks were completing an orbit that would bring them directly overhead. I paused and watched their flight, a close-bunched formation of gracefully flapping wings. In soft tones, the ducks jabbered among themselves. They passed overhead, and I resumed my walk. Three steps on, a salvo of fresh duck manure rained from the sky, splattering around me like a burst of soft hail. I stopped and looked at the fading formation. Chuckling, I was reminded of the time I was live trapping red squirrel from Amarillo's Veteran's Hospital. Officials there complained that they had too many of the little animals, and asked if I would help in relocating some of them. I was placing the squirrels in male-female pairs in city parks that had few. One afternoon, I lifted an entrapped squirrel high above me to check the frightened animal's sex. Just as I was trying to get a closer look, the little rascal urinated at me and almost got me in the face. I laughed at the creature's resourcefulness. Watching the ducks fly away, I marveled at nature's directness. No manipulating or game playing, but rather a straight shot. I had disturbed the ducks, and they made their point. Chuckling again, I walked on and climbed my hill.

I found Her Majesty and Sandose sat side by side in the winter sun, on the chalky cliff ledge. Her Majesty stretched her wing and leg, extending both over the ledge's edge. She spread her fingers, separating her five primary feathers. Her sheen radiated more than I had ever noticed. The whoosh of an approaching flock of cedar waxwings caught her attention. Both eagles watched the gray birds pass. The female retrieved her wing and went through her stowing ritual. From somewhere downcanyon, a coyote howled. Its eerie wail echoed the chasm's walls. I turned toward the sound. From another direction, several other prairie wolves answered the first. Rising in volume, the coyotes squealed, yelped, barked, and howled in a discordant concert. As abruptly as they began, the animals clipped their symphony short, as on some unseen conductor's signal. It was almost as if they had been singing about what a nice hunt they had had, with each coyote telling about the fat rat or rabbit it had caught, or missed, up on the flat. Across the canyon, Her Majesty launched. Instantly, Sandose also pushed from the cliff and followed the female. I'd never seen him fly so close to her before.

I was surprised when the hen eagle landed on another ledge a couple of hundred yards along the canyon. I was further surprised when Sandose landed with her. They sat a moment, and Her Majesty flew again. Again, the tiercel flew close to her. A hundred yards on, the female landed again. Again, Sandose landed with her. They sat only a moment, and Her Majesty flew. The male flew about as close to her as he could.

The two eagles flew their new tip-to-tip flight through a few more landings before wheeling aloft and into hunting formation. Wanting a better seat, I quickly hiked up the rim of south wall behind me.

Twenty minutes later, the widow flushed a cottontail from a cholla cactus. Immediately, the male dove. An instant ahead of the tiercel's talons, the rabbit scurried under a small cedar. The male zoomed back up to a hundred feet and hovered. The widow landed and flogged the cedar. The rabbit held ground. The widow danced around the bush, poking her head in at intervals. When the rabbit didn't flush, I presumed the rodent had gone to ground, as fox hunters say when their quarry holes up.

Her Majesty lumbered back into the air, and the two eagles

resumed hunting. Within ten minutes, the pair roused a jack-rabbit from somewhere. The rabbit tore across the land, widening its gap between the birds. The hen held back. The tiercel began a climbing circle above the rim, keeping the running jackrabbit in view by looking over or under his wing. At three or four hundred feet, the tiercel leveled and sailed away from the rabbit. The rabbit reduced its escape effort to occasional hops. The hen rose fifty feet above the rim and faced into the canyon. Here she hovered and gently flapped, as though trying to distract the distant rabbit's attention from the tiercel. Sandose continued sailing away. The jackrabbit stopped and tentatively nibbled prairie grass, casually glancing toward the female eagle.

When the tiercel was probably only a minor speck in the sky to the rabbit, or nothing at all, Sandose backed his wings and made a gradual turn, away from the prairie and out over the canyon. The rabbit continued to munch, either not seeing the male eagle or unconcerned about it. As far as I was concerned, the jackrabbit was about to become an eagle pellet.

Sandose made a sweeping turn, gradually backing his wings more as he came about. When the eagle straightened, I reasoned, it probably reached a point that placed a thick cedar between its small image and the rabbit. Sandose tracked the rabbit's direction, at the same time accelerating in a long, shallow dive. I estimated the bird's speed at between sixty or seventy miles per hour. I also noted the eagle was attacking crosswind, which would reduce chances the rabbit might hear wind-harping eagle wings.

The jackrabbit hopped a casual hop, paused, and munched. Her Majesty held position. Sandose sped on. Two hundred yards from an especially fat cedar, the bird curved up, just enough for a quick peek above the bush. Just as quickly, he dipped back below the bush top enough to remain hidden. Fifty yards from the cedar, the eagle trimmed its flight to skim the tree's upper edge, roared past the plump cedar, and dipped, apparently to blend his streamlined profile into the bush's background.

"Goodbye bunny," I whispered. Then I became alarmed.

Sandose was closing so rapidly on the rabbit, I calculated he might not be able to break his speed in time. Suddenly, the jackrabbit flattened in the grass and flicked its ears, up once and down. The eagle bore on. Then, at the last possible second, the rabbit burst from the grass and scampered across the prairie. Roaring on, the tiercel clinched his feet into fists, drew near, rotated, and jabbed. The rodent tumbled end over end across the prairie. Sandose zoomed up, and turned sharply back. The rabbit wobbled to its feet. The eagle dove and bound to the dazed rabbit. Her Majesty turned and flew low over the prairie, toward the grappling tiercel.

The widow landed a few feet away from the male bird. The jackrabbit kicked grass and dust into the air, jerking Sandose across the prairie and forcing him to use his wings and tail for balance. After a moment, the rabbit ceased struggling. The tiercel looked at the female, quickly spread his tail fan, and cupped his wings forward, to the ground, hiding his catch. I shook my head, thinking, "Dummy." One of the rabbit's feet spasmed from under his feathers. Instantly, Sandose expanded his wing over the errant leg. After it was quiet a moment, the tiercel ducked his head under his feather screen. Looking like a headless eagle, he was apparently studying his catch, as a poker player scrutinizes new cards. "Little stink," I thought, and I wondered if he'd ever come to realize Her Majesty was part of the hunt. His head came up. Sandose looked at Her Majesty. The eagle stood still. The tiercel slowly retracted his wings. The jackrabbit lay motionless. Sandose bent his eyes to his catch and raised his head again. Slowly, he relaxed his grip from the rodent's rib cage and stepped aside. Her Majesty took a cautious step forward. Sandose stood still. The female clamped one claw around the rabbit's abdomen, and hooked her beak into its rib cage.

From my seat across the canyon, I applauded Sandose. When I raised my glasses again, both birds were staring at me. I waited until they turned back and applauded again. Again, they stared. Mentally, I noted, "Eagle ears are as good as eagle eyes." A moment later, Her Majesty resumed feeding. I felt like applauding once more but skipped it.

After the eagles fed, they perched and began preening. I checked my watch. It was almost time for me to go to work. With the few minutes I had left, I watched them work their feathers. As soon as they finished, Her Majesty flew. That surprised me, since I had come to know her to sit a while when her crop was full. Again, Sandose flew with her, holding that unusually close formation, following her every move. His flight reminded of my own formation flying, a type requiring precise attention. When the birds neared the rim, that twittering flock of cedar waxwings came undulating along. Suddenly, Sandose broke away from Her Majesty and rushed toward the small birds. Speeding, he dove through the swarm, scattering waxwings like chaff in a March wind. After he passed through their flight, the small birds quickly reassembled and twittered on their way. Sandose climbed back toward Her Majesty. Halfway to her, he again diverted, this time to dive on a pair of black ravens, apparently en route to some canyon destination. The ravens scattered, croaking displeasure, and flew on. The tiercel turned and climbed again toward the hen.

The eagles circled aloft. When they were high above the canyon, the two-eagle formation danced in the sky, twisting, turning, diving, climbing, and spiraling. Halfway around a sharp turn from medium altitude, Her Majesty interrupted her flight, leveled her wings, backed them, and aimed a new direction. Sandose followed. Her flight reminded me of previous owl chasing flights. I panned ahead of the diving-eagle formation.

Across the canyon, a lone owl flew along the cliff's winter shadow. The owl flew as though unaware the eagles were about. The eagles rushed on. In a moment, however, the owl leisurely turned into its finger canyon, well ahead of the speeding eagles.

The owl disappeared into the tall tree. Her Majesty checked her dive and made a sweeping turn back toward the rim. Sandose stayed right with her. When they reached north rim, they circled aloft once more. At three hundred feet, Her Majesty leveled. From the way she flew, I suspected what she was about to do.

For a long time, the female eagle held steady. Sandose also held steady, only inches from her wing tip. At last, Her Majesty closed her wings, dropped rapidly to the rim, and snatched a baseball-sized rock. Quickly, she rose back to the tiercel. She inched next to him, looked at him, and dropped her rock. Sandose bent his head down and watched the stone fall. When the rock was half-down, he tentatively folded his wings and dove a few feet. The stone struck the ground and clattered over the rim. Immediately, Her Majesty plunged to the rim, snatched another rock, and rose. Next to the male, she stabilized once more. Sandose twisted his head, and looked at the rock that was clutched in Her Majesty's dangling talons. She opened her foot. The rock fell. Instantly, Sandose folded and dove.

XIV

SANDOSE BARELY CAUGHT THE ROCK before it reached the rim. If I hadn't been holding my binoculars with such determination, I'd have applauded again. Slowly, the male eagle climbed. His rock-holding leg dangled. The bird climbed aimlessly, as though uncertain. Her Majesty seemed patient. At last, he reached their original altitude and slipped into position next to her. After hesitating, he glanced at her and released the rock. The she eagle spiraled after the tumbling rock, wildly and happily. Halfway down, she snagged it. With seeming purpose, she circled back up. From just off his wing tip, and perfectly stabilized, she snapped open her talons. Instantly the tiercel retracted his wings and dove.

Sandose caught the rock easily. This time, he climbed as if he knew what he was about. At her altitude, he stabilized, looked at Her Majesty, and released. The she eagle dove and caught. Quickly, I glanced my watch. If I were going to meet my obligation to the studio, I had no choice but to leave. Reluctantly, but happy inside, I left my post and walked toward home.

On the way to Currie headquarters, I kept looking back at the eagles. They continued their game of aerial catch. Within a short distance, however, I was forced to choose between eagle watching, or getting home without stumbling. Irritated, I chose the latter.

As I drove to town, I pondered the eagle's rock dropping game. What would come next? I wondered. It's my experience that in nature, there's purpose for everything. I suppose this is one reason

I enjoy nature. She's honest. I like that. And I planned to be in the canyon to rub shoulders with her honesty again early tomorrow.

Daylight was breaking when I pulled on my coat and gloves, gathered binoculars and a plaid wool blanket, and stepped outside. It was cold, which my fifty-thousand-dollar hunch told me last night it should be. Wind drift indicated the eagles would fly the north rim's upslope today. In the VW, I drove toward south prairie. Near a rocky point, I parked and walked to a red rock jut suspended in the canyon's airspace. I sat down on the jut's edge and dangled my feet into the canyon. The gorge's floor was about two hundred feet below. The rock was as cold as New Year's football stadium seats. I draped the blanket over and under my legs.

"All I need now," I mused, "is popcorn and hotdogs." I scanned the yellow cliff. The eagles weren't there. I searched other cliffs. No sign of Sandose or Her Majesty. Presuming the eagles were perched on my side of the canyon, out of sight, I settled back. The back of my canyon seat was no more accommodating than a stadium's. Wishing for popcorn, I hungered and waited.

The top edge of the sun burned through the eastern horizon. I knew what the answer would be but checked my watch anyway. Exactly three minutes later, the sun's full disc perched on the horizon. Those predictable three minutes made me secure in the knowledge that, in spite of last night's news, the world was still in order, still spinning right on schedule. Nature's honesty was reconfirmed. I took a deep breath, cool and fresh. Below, a bluebird flashed. Then another. Across the canyon a coyote howled, and I guessed I was announced. I raised my hand and said, "Good morning, coyote." Downcanyon, a group of the little prairie wolves suddenly sang. After the second chorus, the coyotes suddenly ceased, and the canyon was quiet again.

Half an hour after sunrise, Sandose and Her Majesty flapped

from somewhere on the south side of the canyon, to north rim. The birds rose and hunted. When Sandose finally stooped, his dive was away from the canyon, terminating about a mile back from the rim. I guessed he caught from the fact that he didn't reappear and also that Her Majesty landed about where he went down. When she didn't come back up, I was reasonably sure Sandose shared.

It was an hour before I saw the birds again. They were high in the morning sky and rising. At about fifteen hundred feet, the eagles cavorted in close formation. Sometimes the female led, at other times the male led. After one dive and pullout, Sandose rolled on his back, underneath Her Majesty. Their talons touched briefly, the tiercel's wings flashed in the sun, and he completed his roll, turning upright beside the hen. I was surprised to see a bird roll upside down and around. Aeronautically, he did a barrel roll, and I was eager to drop this eagle lore into the conversation of a group of flight instructors grounded by a rainy day.

The birds continued playing in the sky. A few minutes later, Sandose rolled under the hen again, touched her talons, completed his roll, and flashed up beside her. The two birds chirped to each other, and Her Majesty turned upcanyon. She backed her wings and slanted into a long, descending track. Sandose trimmed to a flight regime identical to hers and followed. "What's next?" I wondered.

The female traveled perhaps a mile, leading the male to a peculiar flat-topped cedar. The cedar was near the point where she seemed to have drawn her territory line in the past. Just above the cedar, she faced into the canyon, hovered, deployed spoilers, and landed in the bush's top. The tiercel turned and hovered over her. Her Majesty sidestepped to the right side of the bush, using her wings for balance. Resettled, she stowed her wings. Sandose dropped lightly to the bush beside her. After a brief moment, the hen eagle stretched her neck to a sprig that violated the bush's flat profile. She clamped her beak on the sprig, twisted it away, and dropped it. The tiercel watched the sprig tumble through the bush, then he selected a sprig marring his side and twisted it away. They sat quietly. Then the hen eagle slowly bowed, flattening her back. Nervously, Sandose opened and closed his wings; he opened and closed them again, then held them open. Like a butterfly, he lifted into the air, and floated just over Her Majesty. She gathered her tail fan to one side. Sandose gently settled on her back.

For fifteen or twenty seconds, the eagles copulated, manipulating their wings in the breeze for balance. Finished, the tiercel lifted back into the air, and softly landed beside her. Her Majesty roused and shook her feathers. That done, she spread her wings, rose, and led Sandose straight across the canyon. At a weathered cedar post on the south rim, she landed again. While the tiercel flapped above her, she again bowed and gathered her tail fan. Sandose settled on her back, and again the eagles copulated. When they finished, Her Majesty led Sandose back across the canyon, to north rim's upslope winds. Here, they rose and freewheeled a series of aerial dance patterns. Swooping dives followed breathtaking climbs, slow motion wingovers, and new dives. As they flew, the birds chirped back and forth, causing me to imagine that they were saying to each other, "I like being with you."

From medium altitude, the eagles turned downcanyon. With slightly backed wings, the female again led. After a couple of miles, near the point of that invisible line that seemed to separate her from her neighbors, she hovered above a bare-limbed, gnarled cedar. The neighboring pair of eagles sped toward the tree from their part of the canyon. Sandose rose, as if to protect Her Majesty. The neighbor tiercel flew a mock attack at Sandose. The young tiercel held his ground. At the last moment, the neighbor turned away. With deliberation, Her Majesty landed in the gnarled tree. As soon as she was perched, Sandose sank toward her. Instantly, the neighboring tiercel dove on Sandose again, thrusting talons as he passed. Sandose flapped after the neighbor. Her Majesty flew and made a wide, slow circle. On the other side of the tree, the neighboring hen flew a similar circle, edging her turns near that imaginary line between them. The line seemed to border on the cedar. Occasionally, the males feinted at each other, acting as though they intended to cross. Yet they didn't. At an altitude I estimated to be three or four thousand feet, the male eagles leveled and faced into the canyon. The birds were no more than twenty-five yards apart. After standing off several minutes, Sandose gradually descended. The neighbor tiercel matched Sandose's descent but kept a few feet higher. As the two eagles reached low altitude, Her Majesty reapproached the tree and landed. The tiercels continued descending. When Sandose was low, he approached and landed beside Her Majesty. The neighboring pair continued circling and watching. After a moment, Sandose spread his wings, lifted, and hovered just above Her Majesty. The eagles mated, longer than before. The neighboring pair continued orbiting, as if on station. Suddenly, I had a theory about the importance of the eagle's mating geography.

Was it possible Her Majesty, in her unique way, was showing Sandose the limits of her territory? Seemed reasonable, since the tiercel has no way I could see of knowing what land she considers hers. Certainly her way of defining her territory borders, if this is the case, should impress Sandose. I decided if I were a male eagle, I'd be impressed. Then I sobered on the thought that our pudding's proof lay in seeing if Sandose defended these limits of their sexual tour. Sandose lifted from her and resettled. The neighboring pair continued circling. I glanced from the eagles to the flat-topped bush upcanyon. The distance was about three miles. If Her Majesty claimed a mile and a half either side of the canyon's center, plus a fraction, that would equal ten square miles.

The eagles rose, and I further calculated that from the center of such a territory, the eagles would never be more than 2½

minutes from any border or corner. The birds backed their wings
and headed straight across the canyon. The neighboring pair also
flew across, remaining on their side of the imaginary line. At
south rim, Her Majesty landed on a solid, red jut. Here, she
mated with Sandose again. When they finished, the two eagles
sat side by side. The neighbor eagles hovered, continuing to stay
on their side. After sitting a time that seemed socially appropriate,
Her Majesty flapped from the rock, back to north rim. Sandose
followed in close formation. The she eagle led back upcanyon.
She sailed on and on, at last landing on the flat-topped bush.
Here, she bowed, and the eagles mated again. I replayed my
theory, liking it more and more. No sooner had I finished my
thought than a stray eagle came, approaching flat-top bush.

The new eagle sailed down the rim, flying along as if knowing where it was going. Sandose and Her Majesty launched,
rose, and hovered four hundred feet above the bush. The new
eagle came on. The nearer it came, the higher Sandose and Her
Majesty rose. When it was obvious the cruising eagle intended to
pass the bush, Sandose folded his wings and plummeted like a
fighter at the would-be intruder. The strange eagle made an
evasive turn, out over the canyon. Sandose matched the bird's
course change and plunged on, as though intending to ram the
interloper. The new eagle flapped away, heading back upcanyon.
I smiled, deciding I liked the way eagles marked their territory
better than suburbanite fence building. Just beyond the bush,
Sandose checked his dive and zoomed up in a spiral that repositioned him next to Her Majesty. Both birds hovered above their
conjugal bush. The would-be intruder stopped flapping, angled to
the rim, turned into the wind, and full spanned. The eagle was
equal in size to Her Majesty. A white band marked its tail feathers.
The girl eagle rose to an altitude equal to Sandose and Her
Majesty. Slowly then, she drifted toward them. "Sandose," I said.
"I think you're going to be tested."

The young female continued drifting to a point a hundred yards from Sandose. Here, she partially closed her wings, dropped to the rim, clawed a stone into her talons, and climbed. With her rock-carrying leg dangling, the young she eagle inched close to Sandose and dropped her stone. Sandose stretched his neck and watched. The stone fell, hit the rim, and bounced away. I chuckled, noting all seemed to be fair in love and war in the eagle world, too. The young female dropped to the rim again, stabbed another stone, carried it aloft, and inched closer than before. Her Majesty eased next to her new mate. The girl bird released her rock. Sandose didn't move. After a long pause, the immature female made a slow, climbing circle to her right, away from the paired eagles. Sandose matched her climb. Below and behind him, Her Majesty followed.

The young female continued climbing, with Sandose and Her Majesty matching her spiral for spiral. At what I guessed was about three thousand feet, the young lady eagle shortened her wings, pulled in her neck, accelerated, and tracked straight into Sandose's and Her Majesty's territory. The pair took escort positions on the intruder, and the three eagles tracked a line paralleling the rim, flying downcanyon. At about half a mile from a vertical line above the gnarled cedar, the neighboring pair waited. The traveling trio flew on toward the waiting eagles. When the intruder neared the neighboring pair, she circled. Here, the five eagles milled in slow motion, a high altitude kaleidoscope of wings in the blue. Then the young female dove from the group. After only a short dive, she pulled up, arced into a climb, slowed, twisted into a wingover—dove, rocketed up, slowed, and wingovered. I concluded she was now flirting with the neighbor tiercel. "She probably has a bunch of lice," I mused.

After one more flirting dive and climb, the young girl eagle headed back up the rim where she had come from. Again she was escorted by Sandose and Her Majesty. Above the flat-topped bush, the pair broke off. The young eagle flew on, gradually descending. "Win a few, lose a few," I observed. At the same time, I felt sure I'd soon be counting Sandose's and Her Majesty's eggs.

XV

E ARLY IN JANUARY, Douglas returned to the panhandle on two
weeks leave. It was his last before shipping overseas. I
brought him up to date on the eagles. He was particularly proud
of Sandose, and rightly so, I felt. I wished him luck in his new assignment and agreed to keep him posted.

Through the rest of January and into February, Her Majesty
and Sandose mated several times each day. In addition to copulat-
ing on their territory markers, the eagles also used random spots
on both sides of the canyon rim, but always between those markers. Near the end of February Her Majesty looked heavier, and
her flight was labored. Those observations prompted me to do
research in Amarillo's public library on eagle eggs. With the help
of librarian Aleta Burch I gathered an armload of natural history
and bird reference books and carried them to a table. According
to one reference, eagle eggs weigh 4 to 4½ ounces each. Two
eggs are common in 66 percent of eagle nests; 14 percent hold
three, and on rare occasions a hen lays four. Beyond that, my
eagle research became confusing yet intriguing. One reference
said, "golden eagle eggs are spotted brown." Another said, "all
white." About incubation, one source said the length of time is
thirty days. Another said forty-six. Yet another proclaimed thirty-
five days as proper incubation interval. With widening eyes, I
read that the female eagle performs the entire incubation, while
another source claimed the male eagle shared egg-warming duties.
About young birds' fledgling time, one author wrote, "The young

eaglets flew in nine weeks after hatch." Another writer vouched for eleven; still another, twelve. I chuckled at this conflicting information on golden eagles, but not in disrespect. I chuckled because I was happy to get any answers to these unknowns.

I did, however, find one piece of information that was familiar: "Frequently the larger, stronger nestling kills its younger nestmate while they are still young." This piece labled that event as the "Cain-Abel Battle." I was heartened to discover a common fact between myself and previous eagle watchers. With tweaked curiosity, I returned the nine volumes and searched another source.

From the *Harvard Classics* I found amusing remarks about eagle denotes the Ascension of Christ, immortality, and Saint searched the Bible dictionary and read all ten eagle references. One of the more noteworthy was: "In Christian symbolism, the eagle denotes the Ascension of Christ, immortality, and Saint John." Aha. My first clue as to why some people, without rational explanation, hate and despise the eagle or love the bird. Another quote, not in direct reference to the eagle but one I like, came from Job: "Who teaches us more than the beasts, or makes us wiser, than the fowls of heaven?" I paused there in my research and decided if there is such a thing as reincarnation, I want to come back as an eagle. When I was a kid, I thought to be a quail would be ideal. I must have been impressed with the hot rod takeoff of a quail, their explosive acceleration, and that long, fast glide. I suppose speed, or the illusion thereof, attracted my attention to thinking a quail would be a good bird to be. Now, I appreciate the eagle's command of his life and his world.

I next turned to the *National Geographic's* file for an eagle article I recalled from some time back. The September 1967 issue carried "Sharing the Lives of Wild Golden Eagles," by John, Charles, and Derek Craighead. Early on, the article states, "much of what has been said or written about the golden eagle is merely legendary." I smiled. Between paragraphs, a heading announced,

"Female is larger and more deadly." No explanation was given in the text as to why the size differential between male and female eagles. Deeper into the article, I learned Jerry McGahan discovered from a study of thirty-eight nests that eagles feed their young a diet of 70 percent rabbit, 12 percent assorted birds, and 18 percent diversified small animals and snakes. At the article's end, mention was made that in 1962 Congress amended the Eagle Act of 1940 with Public Law 87884, entitled "The Protection of Bald and Golden Eagles." The law carries fines as high as five thousand dollars and is no doubt the same which Douglas had told me about. However, the law further reads, "On request of the Governor of any state, the Secretary of the Interior shall authorize the taking of golden eagles for the purpose of seasonally protecting domesticated flocks and herds." The eagle-sheep myth marcheth on. I shook my head. At the article's end, a footnote referred to, "In Quest of the Golden Eagle, May 1940." From the reference librarian, I requested that copy from storage.

"In Quest of . . ." was as advertised. The article was the story of the author ranging across lofty, oxygen-thin mountain cliffs, misty escarpments, and ten-thousand foot vertical rock faces. Through the author's eyes we look for eagles but find only a distant few. As I closed the magazine, the librarian brought a copy of the San Angelo (Texas) *Standard Times*. The paper was from Sunday, January 8, 1978. The issue carried a special supplement titled "The Eagle and the Lamb," apparently an outgrowth of a San Angelo sheep rancher's helicopter killing of eagles. The supplement was sponsored by 101 Tom Green county merchants. Folks with a different view about eagles reported the killings to federal wildlife officials. A community-splitting trial resulted. Eagerly, I read on.

The guts of the article was: A lamb had been tied on a fifteen-foot tether; a hidden *Standard Times* photographer waited. A photo showed the lamb stretched to the end of its tether and laying on the ground. I was reminded of the peregrine's natural attraction to the awkwardly flapping duck and Lauri Rapala's artificial minnow with built-in swimming flaw. The next photo showed a golden eagle sitting on top of the lamb. A series of photos followed. These photos were captioned to say the eagle was attacking the lamb. In each of the pictures, I noted the eagle's talons were always outside the lamb's woolly coat and were too small to encircle the animal's body. Unless San Angelo golden eagles were different from panhandle varieties, I was reasonably certain the eagle in the photograph had discovered the toughness of lamb skin and the size of lamb forms. The next picture showed the eagle flapping away. This photo's caption claimed the eagle was alerted to flee by camera sounds. The cutline intimated the lamb had been killed. However, I noted the lamb had moved since the previous picture. My suspicion is the lamb probably jumped up after the eagle left. I turned the page.

The next photo showed a rancher holding a lambskin to the sky. Holes in the skin were alleged to have been made by eagle talons. I smiled, hoping the tax man based in San Angelo wasn't easily fooled. I reassembled the paper, returned it to the librarian, thanked her, and drove for Currie Ranch.

Driving home, I counted myself lucky to have warm and cozy Palo Duro Canyon as an eagle lab. Egg color I was fairly sure I could handle. And fledge time didn't worry. Nor did the question of whether both birds share incubation duties. But how was I to accurately determine eagle egg incubation time?

February's last Saturday came in with forty degree fog and drizzle but no wind. Wrapped in my blanket, I sat on the edge of the red rock jut. Across the canyon, the tiercel was flying. His flight pattern was of the hunt. Her Majesty, however, followed, apparently not directly involved. Considering her "condition," that seemed logical. Sandose flapped from bush to bush, along north rim, to flat-top bush. Here, he turned, crossed the canyon, and worked south rim, back toward me. The eagles veered around me. A quarter-mile past, the male suddenly dove into the canyon and bound to a cottontail in long grass on second level. High-pitched rabbit distress cries echoed off canyon walls. While Sandose squeezed the struggling rabbit, he was forced to use his wings for balance. Suddenly a tan kit fox bounded toward Sandose and the screaming rabbit. I guessed the fox had responded to the rabbit's distress cries. The little animal stopped a few yards away and watched. Shortly, the rabbit's cries ended. Sandose raised his hackles, mantled, and glared at the fox. The hen circled down and landed beside the tiercel. The fox turned, sauntered a few yards, stopped, and looked back. The cottontail quivered. Sandose tightened his grip. Unconsciously, I massaged my left arm. Her Majesty eyed the rabbit. The rodent convulsed again, and again Sandose increased his squeeze. Then, both rabbit and tiercel were quiet a moment. The fox walked on and melted into the canyon. Sandose slowly relaxed his grip and stepped back. The female eagle waddled to the lifeless cottontail, grasped its limp body in one foot, bent her head, hooked her beak into its rib cage, carved lungs and heart out, and gulped them.

When the birds flew, Her Majesty struggled to get airborne. Once she was in the air, she flapped hard to stay there. My mind shifted into high as to why nature may have designed female eagles larger than male eagles. If she were carrying three nearly ready eggs, her weight could be nearly an extra pound. It was likely she also had an extra pound of prebrood fat. A precise ratio exists between an airframe's structural strength requirements and its payload. To increase an aircraft's payload by a few pounds requires additional airframe materials. This aeronautical law is so unbendable, it applies equally to airplanes and birds. For Her Majesty to safely fly with her extra pounds, she needs a bigger body and stronger landing gear. Her larger size satisfies my belief that in nature, there seems to be a reason for everything. And considering the eagle's hunting style, it appears the birds understand inherent advantages in each other's size as far as hunting role assignments go. Facetiously, I wondered how a radical feminist would react to the apparent rigid role structuring in the eagle's male-female division of labor. And then I wondered, why has nature designed men and women differently sized? A specific reason?

Sometimes I wish I could lay back and let the world rotate without pondering why, or without trying to imagine what would happen if it didn't. But generally, my curiosity won't let me, probably because of mom's influence in my young years. This was one of those non-laid-back times. "Why are men and women unequally sized?" I asked myself again. To go back to man's early history seemed a logical beginning, so I imagined a caveman environment.

My mind's eye pictured a lone, animal-skin-clad male, sitting just inside a cave, roasting leg of venison. Six inches of new snow covered the countryside. I then shifted my mind's eye to a point five miles away, to a half-starved female, desperately chasing a small deer, without success. Exhausted, she pauses to rest. I imagined her stomach rumbling, and saw her brush hair from her face. In the distance, she spots smoke from the caveman's fire. Driven by hunger, she stumbles toward the smoke. Then I imagined that an hour later she is peering from behind a bush, a hundred yards from the caveman. The man is sitting against a rock beside his fire. A tattered skin he has been repairing lays beside him. His feet are crossed, and he is picking roast venison from his teeth. His unfinished roast lay on a rock beside him. The woman rushes forward, grabs the roast, runs a few yards, and ravenously eats. Then my imagination advanced a couple of hours. I pictured the caveman and the female sitting together before the fire, in the afterglow of an evening both had found pleasurable. Under the spell of their shared evening, they decide it would be mutually advantageous to remain together, agreeing she could keep the fire and tan raw hides into clothing, while he would make bows and arrows and hunt. "An instant family," I mused, then wondered if our man-woman size differential was purposely designed by the creator, to force man-woman dependency? Interesting idea, I thought, and considered it might be valid in a snowbound caveman era. However, snowbound caveman circumstances seem stacked against females, making them more dependent on a male partner for survival than vice versa. The word "dependency" made me frown, until I modified it into "dependency skills." Yes, the dovetailing of caveman-cavewoman skills that founded a mutually beneficial relationship. But we're out of the caves, I reminded, and asked myself, "So what about today?" Well, I thought, modern technology has provided women an easier survival chance. In a sense, our hunting grounds are now within the corporation and factory. Here, a woman may hunt on a par with a man, and she can choose to be independent of his help if she wants. Mutually beneficial male-female dependency skills diminished under modern technology. A clue to modern family's restlessness, and subsequent divorce rate? Wistfully, I wondered if my personal male-female relations might be even more rewarding if our male-female role assignments were based on *Homo sapiens* survival values, instead of our cultural pressures.

By late afternoon the fog lifted and the drizzle diminished. The two eagles sat on the chalky peak ledge, digesting and preening. At about four o'clock they flew. From somewhere near the birds, a sparrow hawk chattered. I raised my binoculars in time to see the little hawk flash past the hen. Jabbering, the hawk climbed, turned, and slanted into a flapping dive at Her Majesty. The tiny bird shrieked down and swooped over her. The lady eagle glanced over her shoulder, sideslipped, and batted her ponderous wing at the passing kestrel. Sandose rose toward the midget hawk. The little hawk screamed, yo-yoed up, and dove on the male eagle. Several yo-yos and a quarter-mile on along the rim, the hawk broke off and let the eagles cruise in peace.

At about the middle of their territory, the eagles rose above the rim, turned into the wind drift, and spread their wings full sail. At two or three hundred feet, the hen backed her wings and aimed for south rim. The tiercel folded his wings, dropped, and landed on the cliff below him. Apparently, he was watching his mate. Her Majesty continued crossing. When she was reasonably near, I lowered my binoculars and watched unaided. The eagle seemed to be tracking for the draw holding the aerie she had used last year. A couple of hundred yards from the draw, her flight path arched up. A few yards in front of the gray rock cave, she backflapped and landed.

Last year's nest was now a disarray of weathered sticks. Her Majesty lowered her head and clumsily moved inside. The eagle stood still, looked around, and stepped to the front. At the lip, she dove off and flapped away. I was surprised when she tracked upcanyon, toward me, rather than across the canyon. She came on, paralleling south rim, getting closer. I focused my binoculars on the male. He was sitting there, seemingly watching her. I came back to Her Majesty. She had set up a landing approach. In front of a slanting cliff, she backflapped and landed on a narrow ledge. I looked closely. The female eagle had landed on a collection of old sticks laid under a small overhang. The spot was near her favorite gray shelf perch. I was amazed at not having noticed the sticks before.

In a moment, the hen eagle flew again, heading back downcanyon. Quickly, I checked Sandose. He was slowly turning his head, as though following. I swung back to the former widow eagle. She passed the cave nest and flew on. Near the far edge of her territory, she landed on another nest. This aerie was on a high, red rock face. The nest was not more than ten feet below the rim. Her Majesty walked around on the nest's sticks, stood still, looked around, and flew.

During the next twenty minutes, the hen eagle visited five more nests located up and down the canyon. Of the eight total, only one was on the gorge's north side, and it was hidden in the darkness of a narrow fissure in a cliff, behind a tall cedar. Each of the nests would be shaded during most of the day. Through her nest inspection flights, Sandose watched his mate with undivided attention. The fourth and seventh nests were only touched by Her Majesty in quick, passing pauses. The eighth nest she treated differently. She flew four or five different approaches to this nest. The aerie was laid on a tan sandstone ledge thirty or forty feet below the rim and about sixty feet above the canyon floor. A prickly pear cactus was rooted at the nest's base, to one side of center. My guess about her several flights to the nest was that she was checking food delivery routes that might be necessary in different wind situations. Now she was sitting on the aerie. When she sat there over an hour, I presumed she may have been making certain the location was quiet, or safe, enough to raise young eagles. At last she flew, heading straight for Sandose.

Nearing the tiercel, Her Majesty skimmed the rim, snatched a yard-long stick by one end, and flew in front of her mate. Sandose launched and followed. The eagles assembled into tip-to-tip formation, faced the canyon, and rose as high as the clouds allowed. The silhouette of her outstretched wings, combined with the length of her dangling leg and stick, gave the female the appearance of an airborne T. Humorously, I wondered if some Egyptian had carved the eagle's stick-carrying shape into rock, that was later translated into our present alphabet's T. As soon as the tiercel bent his head to inspect her stick, Her Majesty released. Instantly the male eagle closed his wings and dove. Down they went, turning and twisting. At the last moment the male clawed the stick out of the air, spread his wings, and lifted his prize aloft. At the female's level, and stable next to her, he released. The hen dove, plucked the stick out of the air, and headed across canyon, carrying her stick. Compared to a few weeks ago, her flight was labored. Without hesitating, the tiercel set his wings and followed.

On an arrow-straight track, the female led the tiercel toward the tan sandstone cliff nest. Over the stream she leveled, about even with the ledge ahead, and sailed on. A hundred yards from the cliff, she arced up, reduced speed, and increased her arc's curve as she approached the nest. Swooping up from below, she timed the peak of her arc to produce minimum speed at the instant she reached the nest. Rapidly slowing, she rotated her head up, extended her free leg, backflapped, and touched her claw to the nest. Her stick-holding leg helped absorb the small impact of her landing. Sandose landed beside her. Her Majesty clomped into the structure's center, dragging her stick behind. Here she released her stick, bent forward, took a small twig from the nest in her beak, and plopped it, not seeming to care where or how it landed. Tentatively, the male eagle took a twig in his beak, held it a moment, and carefully placed it. That done, he turned, walked to the aerie's lip, dove off, and rowed across the canyon.

At north rim, Sandose landed, gathered a stick in his talon, spread his wings, rose, and recrossed the canyon. Working like a winged beaver, he arranged the nest's sticks, deftly handling large limbs with his feet and smaller twigs with his beak. Her Majesty watched, turning her head this way and that. Occasionally, she clamped a stick in her beak, lumbered over, and plopped it where Sandose worked. The tiercel was so intent, he seemed not to notice her contribution. Every minute or two, Sandose crossed the canyon, gathered new material, and returned. Within thirty minutes, the pile of weathered sticks had been converted into an organized thatch. After pausing a moment to inspect his work, the tiercel trampled the nest's middle, using his wings for balance as he turned circles for complete coverage. Apparently satisfied with that portion of his work, Sandose flew out and again crossed the canyon. Obviously Douglas was right about who builds eagle nests. But why had nature programmed the male to do so?

On the tiercel's return, he carried a bladed, dry yucca root in his right claw. He arranged the yucca near the nest's center, to the left, and he returned with another and then another. His next trip, his claw held a bundle of dry love grass. In the next few minutes, the eagle worked that, and three more loads of love grass, into the aerie's middle. Circling, he arranged the grass then settled himself on it. Rolling first one way then the other, Sandose worked his feet under him. Now and then he rose, shifted his angle of attack, laid on the grass again, and continued working it. At last he stepped from the soup-bowl-sized, love-grass–lined eggcup. He inspected his work and, without cere-mony, flew, leaving Her Majesty standing on the nest's side. Look-ing like a queen, she watched Sandose cross.

As the tiercel turned above the chalky cliff, it occurred to me why the birds may have so many nest sites. Sanitation? Strikes me as reasonable. And it is obvious who in the eagle world picks the site. I suppose that is as it should be, since she will spend the most time there. But I wish she had consulted me. Her new aerie meant I'd have to build a new blind. I studied the area.

About a hundred feet from the nest, a jillion-ton slab of sand-stone had halved from the main cliff. The huge slab angled slightly away from the parent rock, creating an upward-angling fissure. Time and the elements had sifted enough dirt into the fissure to fill it to within about five feet below the top edge of the slab. A few weeds and an occasional prickly pear cactus struggled in the shady earthen floor. The floor was about a yard wide. The parent rock would be my left wall, the slab my right. All I needed to do was plug the front and fashion a roof. Getting into the blind without being seen by the eagle would be a different matter.

Fortunately, the fissure didn't shear straight. About a hundred and fifty feet from the nest, there is a bulge in the break. Away from the nest, the break angled back toward the rim. About two hundred feet from the nest, I could enter the fissure around the obtuse-angled corner of the bulge. I'd have to tie a knotted assist rope, at least forty feet long, down the steep rock, to the fissure's narrow floor. At least it would be an easy blind to build, and I knew I'd build it tonight. Because I was hooked.

After supper, I assembled blind-building material, drove to the cliff, set up shop within two hours, and returned home. Before daybreak, I was back in my new blind. It was clear and cold. Very quietly, I set up the tripod for my motor-driven Nikon. The camera was coupled to a five-hundred–millimeter mirror reflex lens. To reduce the len's glare, I taped a flat, black-painted, one-gallon bean can to the len's normal shade. To deaden the camera's sound, I wrapped its body in a sheepskin jacket I had made in an Amarillo saddle shop. The elevation of my blind was about fifteen feet higher than the nest, which gave me a slight downward view onto the nest platform. In gathering light, I focused. The lens focusing scale said I was 80 degrees from the nest. Her Majesty was laying on the aerie. I couldn't help grinning. Quietly, I eased open a waterproof .50 caliber ammunition can, took out a small, red, daily reminder and a pencil, and I entered on February 25: "In blind 5:55 A.M. HM setting on nest. Presume first egg is under her." I laid the book aside and searched for Sandose.

Through a tiny slit in my wire, burlap, and cedar-branch roof, I focused my binoculars across the canyon. Sandose was perched on the shelf below the peak. A second after I found him, he flew to the peak and landed. Sitting there, he looked as though he would take on a brontosaurus silly enough to set a toenail inside his territory. Sandose may not have been capable of reasoning; nevertheless, he looked as if he knew he was about to have a family.

Within half an hour, the tiercel flew, hunted fifteen minutes, and stooped. In another fifteen minutes, he landed back on his guard peak. His crop bulged. Almost immediately, Her Majesty flew, heading straight for the point where Sandose's stoop ended on the prairie. Quickly I looked through the Nikon's powerful lens. The nest cup held no egg. I frowned. A second later, I heard the swoosh of arriving eagle wings. I peered at the nest again. Sandose stood on the front edge of the aerie.

In a few minutes, Her Majesty was back. Her crop also bulged.

Sandose flew, and she resettled on her eggcup. In my log, I entered: "Since there is no egg yet, I presume mother eagles prewarm their eggcups prior to egg laying." Sandose returned to his guard post.

It seemed logical to me that the eagle would lay her first egg any time. But how I was to know when? Here I had gone to the trouble of watching the birds for months, had built a blind on a cold night, had given up sleep to be back in the blind before it was light, and didn't know for certain how I would know that my efforts were worth it. After a moment's thought, I decided I needed one of three things: Superman's vision; a hole drilled up through rock below and into the nest; or communication with the hen eagle in English so I could ask her to announce the news. Then I remembered brooding chickens have a bare skin patch called a brood patch to press against eggs. Every so often, the hens turn their eggs with the chin side of their beaks to distribute body heat evenly to the eggs. Surly eagles do the same. All I had to do was watch Her Majesty closely enough to catch the first egg turning.

As the day progressed, I discovered eagle-nest watching is a lot like watching grass grow. In contrast to past months, traffic in the canyon was quiet. I suppose the hawks were also nesting and the American eagles had migrated to wherever they go to next. Through morning, Sandose continued to stand guard. Her Majesty just sat. I fought sleep and studied my blind in light of furnishing it with a sleeping arrangement. But that would hardly contribute to my eagle knowledge. So, I fought sleep. Noon came quietly. As the time passed, I yawned, kinked, unkinked, stretched, and sometimes shivered. At one o'clock I flexed my shoulders. By two I had mentally devised a closed-circuit TV setup that would broadcast a picture of the nest to a receiver beside my fireplace. Then, at four-thirty, Her Majesty rose to a half-crouch. Holding her body low over the nest cup, she tucked her head under her breast. In her shadow, I saw an egg. She was turning it. I focused the camera on the egg. My hands shook. With concentrated precision, she half-rolled the light-colored ovum. Her shadow kept me from seeing if it was all white or splotched. But film might see. I pressed the Nikon's switch. Inside the sheepskin, its motor whirred, its shutter clicked, and its mirror slapped. Instantly, Her Majesty scrambled to the nest's lip and flew away. My heart sank.

XVI

As I watched her majesty race away, my throat tightened. At north rim, she swooped up and landed on the edge of a rock cliff. From there, she glared at my blind. I felt guilty and hoped she couldn't see into the semidarkness of my blind. Nearby, the whoosh of eagle wings sounded toward the nest. I shifted. Sandose was stepping to the eggcup. Awkwardly, he belly flopped on the egg. Tears formed in my eyes, and I loved that little tiercel. His tail feathers stuck up in the air, and the primaries of one wing angled up like a ladies hat plume. He faced the rock wall forming the back of the nest. His head and eyes aimed across the canyon. I was proud that he came to cover the eggs but chuckled at his posture. Suddenly, I had a clue to the mystery of why male eagles build eagle nests.

If the female built the eggcup to her size, it would be a sloppy fit for the male. On cold, windy days, that would threaten the security of eagle eggs during the male's brooding turn. The male's brooding turn? I was surprised at how readily I accepted the fact Sandose was apparently going to share egg brooding, in spite of his comical egg posture. Regardless, to assure species *Aquila chrysaetos* continuing survival, it seemed logical that nature should program the smaller eagle to build the nest. But then, another good reason for him to do so lay in the fact of her heaviness and resulting aerial clumsiness with developing eggs. Through the eagles' lives I had observed that whoever is best suited to a task performs that task, without regard to role assignment by sex

125

alone. The fact that they are 180 million years old speaks to their life-style's advantage. Mentally, I compared present-day husband-wife task assignments. Tentatively, I wondered if we are hung up on so-called roles; we may be rowing against a natural tide. Thinking on that, I frowned.

Fifteen minutes passed before Her Majesty returned. Before she landed, Sandose stepped to the nest's front and flew, as though glad to be going. I studied the egg. It was solid cream colored. The two eagles passed in flight, and the hen landed. After a long stare my way, she stepped to the eggcup. She eyed her egg, moved over it, gingerly placed her feet on either side, and settled. With her beak, she tucked grass into her wing-body juncture. Triumphantly, I entered in my log: "Tiercel shares egg brooding. First egg, cream." I felt smug, until a voice within chortled, "So, we've got egg arrival and proof the male shares egg duty. Big deal. Now how do we expect to know exactly when the egg hatches?" I frowned. Not wanting to grapple with the question then, another side answered, "For all we know, Sir Daniel, she may do a dance on the nest, or Sandose may fly loop the loops." But I couldn't kid myself. Precise hatch time proposed a problem.

Content with the results of my eagle-watching day, I unkinked, left the blind, climbed the rock face, and drove for home. High on my list of things to do was have a doubling layer of sheepskin made to silence my camera.

Thirty-six hours after Her Majesty's first egg came, her second arrived. This egg was heavily splotched reddish brown.

Her Majesty turned her eggs every two to four hours. When she resettled, she always rotated her body position 120°, or a third of a circle. Days lengthened, and spring spread through the canyon on the love call of courting dove. Arias of finch, cardinal, and mockingbirds floated from trees and cliffs. New flowers scented the air, and monarch butterflys fluttered back from Mexico; swallowtails twinkled yellow wings among juniper; and Mississippi kites returned, along with scissor-tailed flycatchers, eastern phoebes, and cliff swallows. The eagles settled into a routine. When Her Majesty left the nest to hunt or feed, Sandose took his turn. In addition, he checked into the nest every three or four hours, apparently to see if his mate wished respite. If Her Majesty sat still, he quickly left, as if glad his services weren't yet needed. When the hen accepted his relief, she often detached from her eggs and launched before Sandose reached the aerie. I never saw the male bird turn the eggs, so I presume he was more guard than brooder.

As the weeks passed, I gathered interesting answers to the sex lives of golden eagles. About every other day, when the tiercel came to take his brooding turn, Her Majesty would meet him at midcanyon and would fly back across with him. On the far rim, or on a bush, the pair then mated. As time went on, I suspected the golden eagle may be the second sexiest creature on earth— second only to us. I also noted that after copulation, the tiercel always returned to the nest and took his brooding turn. Invariably, after fifteen or twenty minutes on the eggs, his eyelids inched shut and his head drooped until his beak rested on the nest's sticks. Occasionally he jerked awake, swiveled his head, and searched the canyon. I was amused at how easily the eagle turned its head without moving other parts of his body. Of course, that loose-skinned neck also allowed him to scan for game without moving when perched in a tree. After an hour on the nest, the male eagle's restlessness increased. Those times when the hen was gone up to an hour and a half, he kept his eyes aimed over the open canyon. When he at last spotted Her Majesty, he would step from the eggs and dive, leaving their eggs exposed until she arrived.

Almost every afternoon around three o'clock, I noticed a roadrunner pedal down a game trail on the canyon floor. This particular chaparral had an apparent arthritic right foot, so I knew it was the same bird each day. With its foot doubled into a ball, the little cockatoo gimped along, snapping up a grasshopper here or lizard there. The roadrunner's schedule was so regular, I could nearly set my watch by it. I liked the little bird and most always watched it until it was out of sight. Then, one day in March, strange neighbors moved in below Her Majesty's aerie.

A few feet below the nest, nature eroded several grapefruit-sized holes into the rock. Several pairs of wild pigeons set up nesting in those holes. The plump pigeons came and went with immunity. Although Her Majesty watched them wide-eyed, raising her head high to keep them in sight as they flew under her nest, there was nothing she, or Sandose, seemed to be able to do about them. After watching in amusement a few days, I came to this conclusion about how pigeons are able to raise squabs in the shadow of instant death.

When a fighter plane approaches for landing, wheels and flaps drag in the breeze, and engine power settings are throttled. In that mode, the fighter is stripped of strength. So is Sandose on approaching the nest. Slow, and aerodynamically dirty at that instant, the king of birds is momentarily reduced to a cumbersome, feathered mass that is no match for a darting pigeon. I was especially amused when one plump, gray-and-white pigeon seemed to delight in diving at Sandose the instant before he touched the aerie. Sometimes, that same pigeon fluttered onto the nest's ledge, hopped upon outlaying sticks, and cooed at Sandose. Certainly Sandose wasn't tethered, but the pigeon seemed to sense the eagle was tied to the nest, flawing the predator's normal behavior. The tiercel's reaction ranged from haughty ignoring, to moving his head from side to side glaring at the saucy intruder.

A day didn't pass without my thinking on a way to determine when Her Majesty's eggs hatched. By the last of March, I decided to put a small microphone under the eggcup. A tiny, button-sized mike, connected to a battery-powered tape recorder set in my blind. I would use natural-colored wire for connections. By keying the tape to a known time, I would know exactly when the first cheep squeaked from the hatchling's throat. To make the installation, I selected the middle of a warm day, frightened Her Majesty off, and worked as fast as I could.

On the nest, the eggs were goose-egg-sized. I inserted the mike through a four-foot aluminum tube, wrapped it in a baggie, and taped it to form the tube's tip. Between the top of the rock ledge and bottom of the nest, I inserted the mike end of the tube, aiming for the eggcup.

As the mike neared the cup, I threaded the tube between sticks. When the mike reached the bottom of the cup, I probed fingers through the love grass lining, untaped the mike, and withdrew the tube, leaving mike and wire under the nest. Next I ran the wire along the shelf a couple of feet toward the blind. Here I anchored it with a rock, tied a fishing line to the end of the wire, and tied a rock to the fishing line. Then I threw the rock into the fissure forming the walls of my blind. That done, I scaled back up the cliff, pulled up my ropes, and disappeared. When I reached my blind, Her Majesty was back. As I connected the mike wire to my recorder, I was confident I'd have an answer to eagle egg incubation time.

On some of my watching days, I noticed Sandose make a different flight than usual. He rose straight up, so high that he was above the limit of vision from under my blind's roof. The flight was fairly regular, and he usually returned within ten or fifteen minutes. Each time it happened, my curiosity increased. A little while after I finished connecting the recorder, he left on that straight-up flight again. I was trying to watch him when an eagle-sized bird sailed past my nose, heading toward the aerie. The bird was so near that I heard the harping of its wings, and it startled me. As it went away, I saw the bird was a black vulture. It was the first I'd seen this spring. The vulture spotted Her Majesty as it passed, turned, and orbited tight circles directly in front of her aerie. The hen glared at the vulture and yelped in a plantive voice I'd never heard from an eagle. Unhurriedly, the buzzard circled a couple more times, before lazily resuming its downcanyon flight. At that point, Sandose roared from a dive, buzzed the vulture, and climbed away. The black bird paid little attention. The tiercel, seeming unconcerned, crossed the canyon and landed. I wondered why it had taken Sandose so long to respond to the buzzard's nearness to the aerie, and I decided that tomorrow I was going to watch that straight up flight to its end.

By noon the next day, the sun had warmed the canyon. The gorge had also accumulated several more newly arriving vultures. When Sandose paid little attention to the migrants, I guessed the tiercel knew from experience the scavengers could catch no game, and therefore were no threat. The vulture's presence, however, cluttered the air, forcing me to sharpen my large bird recognition skill. Buzzards, I noted, nearly always fly with a pronounced wing dihedral, giving them a V profile. Eagles, on the other hand, nearly always fly on board straight wings. "V for vulture" became part of my vocabulary. Just after noon, Sandose started that flight. I grabbed my binoculars, scrambled out of the blind and up to the rim.

The male eagle climbed higher and higher. High above the rim, at maybe three thousand feet, Sandose poised, motionless, a tiny brown speck. The bird hung so long, my arms grew tired. I lay back on the ground, put my arms on my chest, and repositioned my binoculars. I had the feeling Sandose was looking right at me.

After a long period, the tiercel drifted downcanyon, as though satisfied I was not an immediate threat to the aerie. Sailing at a steady speed, the eagle flew to a point I thought was above the gnarled cedar. Here, he paused. After a moment, he backed his wings, crossed the canyon, and lazily turned above what should have been the red rock territory marker. After a short pause, Sandose headed approximately back upcanyon. Rather than paralleling the canyon, however, the eagle was diagonally crossing. Minute by minute, the high-flying tiercel held a steady course.

As he crossed the canyon's middle, above the stream, the bird seemed headed for flat-top bush, some mile and a half away.

High above the flat top, Sandose turned, and without pausing, flew straight across the canyon, toward the pole. Above the pole, he made a wide, lazy turn and again headed diagonally across the canyon. This time, the bird pulled in his wings and descended. In a moment, it was apparent Sandose was returning to his peak.

I lowered my glasses and watched. The pattern of his flight reminded me of a rancher riding fence, to check the borders of his spread. I believed Sandose had just flown a territory inspection sortie. Apparently the diagonal X pattern was used to regain altitude on the upslope side of the canyon. Curiosity satisfied, I returned to the blind. Half an hour later, the roadrunner sauntered down the trail. His feathers shown irradiant blues and greens and purples. Gimping along the trail, his head was high. He turned it side to side, paused, swished his tail this way and that, scanned, gimped ahead, and stopped to scan again. Then the bird cocked its head in a determined way, as though inspecting something. Something just off the trail. Cautiously, it gimped into the grass, lowered its head, spread its wings, and poised, motionless, as a bird dog on point. I looked closer. A coiled rattlesnake faced the roadrunner. The snake's rattlers vibrated; its tongue flicked. I fine focused.

The little bird bobbed its head, twitched its tail, and gimped nearer to the serpent. With lightning speed, the rattler struck. Faster than lightning, the roadrunner jerked back. Half the snake's length hit the dust. Quickly, the snake recoiled, a fraction slower than its strike. In that split second of recoil, the roadrunner snapped forward and hammered the top of the snake's head with the tip of his sharp beak. The rattler hissed, buzzed, flicked its tongue, retreated into a coil, and glared. Like a matador shaking his cape, the roadrunner shook his outstretched wings at the reptile. Instantly, the rattler struck again.

Again the roadrunner jumped back. Again, the rattler missed. During recoil, the little bird jackhammered the snake's head. This time, the snake coiled its body over its head, showing only the tip of its snout. Its forked tongue flicked in and out. The little cockatoo danced alluringly close, and shook his outstretched wings. The viper lashed, missed, and recoiled. The roadrunner pounded the snake's head and pounded again. The snake slithered backward, shielding its head under a crook in its neck. The snake made a feeble strike. The roadrunner rammed another blow, dead on target. As though punch-drunk, the snake's reflexes seemed slower. Now the roadrunner gimped along after the re-treating, writhing snake, jabbing almost at will. After a few yards, the snake stopped and slowly writhed in the dirt. The chaparral rested a moment, then gingerly grasped the twisting snake's middle in its beak, heaved the reptile into the air, and slammed it to the ground. The snake landed belly up. Slowly, it rolled right side up. The roadrunner slammed the snake to the ground again. Slower, it righted again. The little bird con-tinued slamming the snake until the reptile remained motion-less. After resting a moment, the roadrunner took the rattler's head in his beak, briefly, held it and gulped eight or nine inches of rattlesnake into its gullet. With the remainder trailing behind, the roadrunner gimped on down the game path. Smiling at the bird, I whispered, "Gimpy, you're a Texas mongoose," and I won-dered how the roadrunner would fare against a cobra. For now, I scored it roadrunners one, rattlesnakes, zero.

I took a deep breath and checked Sandose. He was in place. I turned to Her Majesty. She was in place. I checked my recorder. Ready. All I had to do was wait.

XVII

THE MORNING OF APRIL 4, I listened to the tape from my recorder. There were the sounds of the crackling of eagle feet on the aerie; pigeon coos; wren warbles; eagle beak scraping against eagle eggs; harping of eagle wings when a bird landed; a passing airplane's drone; and the faint howl of a coyote. I reset the machine and waited.

At 10:42, Her Majesty rose, turned her tail toward the canyon, bowed, and muted. Her white mute dribbled on the rock below her nest. This was the first time she had muted from the nest since laying her first egg thirty-nine days ago. Torn between wanting to rewind and listen, or to record, I chose to record.

An hour and a half later, Sandose landed. Her Majesty didn't move. Instead of turning and leaving, the tiercel cocked his head to his mate, one way and the other. He cocked his head again, then turned and flew. Five minutes later he was back. A green cedar sprig was in his beak. He bowed and laid the sprig in front of Her Majesty's breast. Quickly, I rewound the tape and listened.

Again, I heard crackling of eagle feet on the nest. Probably Her Majesty when she rose and muted. But wait. In the background, there was faint cheeping. And cheeping again. With trembling fingers, I reset the machine and punched the record button. Anxious for her to rise again, I sat glued to my camera's eyepiece.

Fifteen minutes later, Sandose returned with a fresh cottontail. Again he cocked his head, listened, and flew. A moment later, he was back, with another green sprig. A few minutes later, the female rose, carefully left her eggcup, waddled to the rabbit, and started feeding. This is the first time I had seen her feed on the nest. I pressed my eye to my camera's viewfinder. There was no chick. In fact, I could not find a crack or pip in either egg. I frowned, thinking maybe the cream egg was pipped on a side I couldn't see. Maybe she would turn them again when she finished feeding. I waited.

Her Majesty resettled without turning her eggs. An hour later, she half-rose and turned them. No pips, no chips, no cracks. I was baffled. I replayed the tape. There was a new sound. I rewound and listened again. Between faint cheeping, there was a single, low, soft note. The note sounded like "bo-ahk." "Probably the mother eagle telling the chick which way is out," I reasoned. Still baffled, I reset the recorder.

The rest of the afternoon, I fidgeted between watching the eagle and listening to new tape. Both cheeping and "bo-ahk" continued. When my time came to leave for work, I didn't want to go; however, I knew I'd be back at sunrise. Just before I was out of the blind, Sandose landed with another green sprig.

At the studio, between waiting for the five-hundred–millibar chart to clear my facsimile recorder, I became more convinced the green sprig Sandose brought was a fence. My reasoning was that for thirty-nine days he hadn't brought a sprig. Now, at the first cheep, a fence. Apparently the cheep stimulated his response. Same for the rabbit. Further, the cheeping apparently locked Her Majesty to the nest.

Sunrise came clear and cool. Her Majesty looked no different. Most of the cottontail had been eaten. The night's tape was more cheeping, and more "bo-ahk." A second white stripe marked rock below the nest. "Come on, lady," I whispered. "Get up, so I can see what's going on."

It was an hour and a half before Her Majesty rose and turned her eggs. Neither was pipped. However, when her head was next to her cream-colored ovum, the she eagle paused. As soon as she resettled, I listened to the recording. There was the usual cheeping and one "bo-ahk." "Maybe the little fellow isn't strong enough to break the shell," I thought. "Maybe he's saying, 'Hey, ma, how do I get out of here, over.' And maybe that 'bo-ahk' is Her Majesty saying, 'This way, junior, over.' "

Each time the mother-to-be eagle turned her eggs, I made an increasingly fidgety entry in my log. It was going on the second day of cheeping. Why so long, I wondered, and I waited. However, there was one comforting fact. The cheeping seemed to be getting stronger. I settled back, deciding I had time to watch one more turning before I went to work.

Sandose landed, paused, flew, and returned with another green bough. At 1:08 the she eagle rose. Carefully, she lifted her feet from the cup, turned, and muted. As far as I could see, the eggs remained unpipped. The hen resettled, and it occurred to me that since the egg started talking, Sandose wasn't into egg sitting. Seemed reasonable. Sexist, maybe, but reasonable. When it was almost time for me to go to work, I had mixed emotions. For the eaglet to cheep so long seemed not right. Maybe it really couldn't break out of its prison for some reason. Maybe I should consider going into the nest and helping. The tiercel came in with a fresh rabbit, released it, grasped the remains of yesterday's, and flew. I checked my watch. I'd have to leave in five minutes. I came back to the nest. A downy, golf-ball sized head was wriggling from under Her Majesty's breast feathers. The little head wobbled up against the mother eagle's breast. The eaglet's mouth opened and closed. Its faint cheeping carried into my blind. I smiled, and entered on April 6 in my log: "Forty-first day, cream egg hatched."

Her Majesty stretched her neck high and turned her head down to her baby. The eaglet thrust its cheeping mouth at her beak. Abruptly, the eagle stood, withdrew her claws from beside the chick and the unhatched egg, and waddled to the cottontail.

With her beak, the mother eagle stripped fur from the rabbit's chest. In the eggcup, her baby's head wobbled. From time to time, the eagle shook her head, flinging fur tufts into the air. The little eaglet grew tired and laid its head down. When the rabbit's chest was plucked clean, Her Majesty hooked into the rodent's rib cage and tore the chest cavity open. She probed her beak inside, extracted a small, bloody morsel, and stepped to her chick. The eaglet's head popped up; its tiny mouth snapped open and shut, cheeping and wobbling. The mother eagle followed the eaglet's mouth, from one side to the other and back, without success. She tried again. Back and forth they swayed, with the eaglet's cheeping rising in both pitch and frequency. At last, the eaglet snagged the morsel's dangling end. Most of the meat hung from the side of its tiny beak. The chick held steady and side snapped at the dangling meat. The piece flew across the nest. Her Majesty retrieved the morsel and tried again. The eaglet swayed, snapped, and scored. After gulping the food, the little bird resumed cheeping.

Unable to hold its head up between bites, the baby dropped to the nest cup's edge. Five more bites filled the new eaglet's crop. Apparently contented, the little fluff snuggled next to the splotched egg, and Her Majesty resettled over her brood. This time, she sat high and fluffed, looking almost like a mother hen. With a nice feeling, I made entries in my log and left for work.

About the eaglet's long cheeping time and Her Majesty's "bo-ahk," I decided that nature designed the little eaglets to become friendly way before they hatch since their parents are equipped with lethal talons that grab small, warm animals and eat them.

Next morning, the splotched egg was talking. It hatched thirty-six hours later, also on its forty-first day. Three days later, the Cain-Abel battle erupted. I filed the older chick's beak, but left the nest cup intact because my heart weakened to the feeling the little birds needed the cup's cozy warmth. "Some other year," I promised. Although the older eaglet, Cain continued trying to wage war, his harmless attacks diminished as the days passed.

At sunrise, April 12, Her Majesty was brooding her young. A little while later, the eaglets awoke and she fed them. Abel got his share, and they slept again. When the rising sun had warmed the canyon, the hen eagle rose from her sleeping chicks. The older eaglet's head lay across the little one. Carefully, she stepped to the nest's front and flew. The eaglets continued sleeping. Across the canyon, she landed, and she copulated with Sandose. Afterward, the eagles preened. When they finished, they sat a few moments, before Her Majesty flew back to the nest. Her flight was light and nimble.

As the days lengthened, and the eaglets' downy layers thickened, the mother eagle spent more time away from the nest. Both she and the tiercel hunted for their growing family. Sparrow hawks invariably dive bombed the eagles when they rose. The pesky hawks usually accompanied their attacks with screaming and chattering, as though announcing the eagle's presence to prairie rabbits. At five or six hundred feet, the hawks broke off, and returned to their cliffs.

Game was so plentiful, the eagles hunted separately. However, only Her Majesty fed their youngsters from game she continued to strip of fur or feathers. When Sandose caught first, she met him at the rim across from the nest and received the food from him in midair, talon to talon, transfer. At about three weeks old, the little birds chirped as soon as they saw either parent across the canyon, sometimes when they were as much as a mile distant. And they kept chirping until Her Majesty landed in front of them.

Rabbits continued to be the eaglet's staple; however, their diet included one skunk, one tiger-striped house cat, one orange house cat, a kit fox, a prairie dog, and an occasional quail or duck.

A thought about animals and birds the eagle catches, kills, and eats: Isn't it possible the balance nature has struck between the eagle's ability to catch, and his quarry's ability to escape, is delicate? It seems that eagles can catch only the unhealthy, the imperfect, the witless. From what I've seen, the birds are no match for faultless game examples. Thus doesn't the eagle function as a breeding control, insuring that only pedigree stock is available to breed and to propagate individual species? So when we admire a quail, or a cardinal, or a fox, isn't nature honestly showing us her best?

The eaglets were now eating about every four hours. They slept between. Wren song livened the canyon, and a variety of butterflies twinkled the air. Below the aerie, pigeons came and went, cooing throughout the day. It was here that I realized Sandose wasn't bringing the green sprigs anymore. Since the little ones chirped at the sight of their parents across the canyon, I guess he sensed the eaglet's eyes had developed enough to see nest edge danger themselves. I further guessed the male's signal to bring a sprig is keyed to the pitch of infant cheep, rather than the pitch of their developing, lower voices. We could test this by placing a speaker in the nest with "fresh" eggs, and playing a recording of infant cheep for the tiercel. Someday.

At the end of the fourth week, the oldest eaglet weighed three pounds, eleven ounces. The second hatchling was eight ounces less. The eaglets ate one-third of their current weight each day. From the first few days after hatch, the chicks were expert at racing backwards to the nest's edge, raising their little rears, and shooting a stream of white mute well clear of the nest. Now, rock below the nest was whitewashed. Smiling, I wondered how their neighbors liked that.

Also at four weeks, along the back edge of the bird's stubby wings, a row of black dots marked emerging flight feathers. At this age, the young eagle's talons were strong enough to grasp food, and they made first attempts at feeding themselves. Although the birds could now stand, their walk was unsteady, forcing them to use their wing stubs for outriggers. Occasionally, the young eagles made stumbling runs across the nest, flailing as they went. At about this same time, I read a newspaper story about eagle egg incubation records on a pair of captive eagles in the Topeka, Kansas zoo. Forty days was given as the period zookeepers discovered. I suppose the difference might be due to the birds being captive.

The eaglets' trampling about the nest eliminated the eggcup, leaving the aerie a level platform. The growing birds' activities created a landing traffic problem for the mother, therefore she began using a specific spot on the nest's front for landings. After a few days, sticks there were mashed into a depression. When Her Majesty was coming from across the canyon, the young birds got well away from that spot. Every now and then a mockingbird landed in this depression, looked at the young eagles, swished its tail, and screeched into the nest. At first the eaglets flattened themselves and lay stone still. In time, however, they learned to rear up, open their beaks, and hiss at their visitor. The mockingbird seemed unimpressed and took its time vacating the landing area.

Between the fourth and sixth weeks, Her Majesty stopped brooding her offspring at night, except when it was extra cool or during storms. Rain, wind, and lightening were accepted by the birds; however, they raised their heads to thunder. During awake periods they either preened, fed, or patiently scanned the rim. Sitting on their haunches with feet sprawled in front, belly protruding between their legs, and stubby wings for outriggers, the birds would search the air. While waiting, the eagles amused themselves watching flies or bugs attracted to rotting meat tidbits. Sometimes wren or brown creepers fed on insects in the aerie's fringes. The eagles' alertness had developed enough that they could tell the difference between the flight of their parents and that of buzzards. And when the birds spotted a parent, they cried in a deep, gull-like, "Yee-app, yee-app, yee-app," that echoed the canyon walls. I came to appreciate their unerring accuracy in announcing that Sandose or Her Majesty were about.

At six weeks, the young eagles had sprouted half their flight feathers, giving them a mottled, half-black–half-white color. Stubby tail fans were developing, and at this age, they pounced nest sticks or jabbed at flies with their claws. The birds were also now strong enough to feed themselves from game that was still stripped.

It was also becoming obvious the first-hatched eaglet was female. Her feet were bigger, her head was bigger, and her body was bigger. The little girl eaglet nearly always outmaneuvered her brother for food, forcing him to watch her feed until she was full. When the girl eaglet won her food scramble, she mantled over her prize. Then, as she fed, the young tiercel pecked at parts that his sister's feathers were too short to hide. At this, the girl bird raised her hackles and hissed. The boy eagle would then turn to nibbling nest sticks or to playing with a bone leftover from previous game. During this period, Her Majesty allowed Sandose to bring food to the nest. Each time a parent brought food, the adult bird carried depleted carcasses away as they left. The most weight either eagle carried into the aerie was 2½ pounds, the weight of a grown cottontail. Jackrabbits were brought in halves, at about 2½ pounds per half.

At eight weeks the young eagles were fully feathered. Their plumage was such a dark shade of brown it was almost black. The birds tail fans were banded white, and white patches colored their wrist joints on the underside of their wings. In addition, a small white patch marked the young bird's crops. When they were fully fed, the eagle's bulging crop turned this white patch out to its maximum. On the other hand, when the young eagle's crops were empty, the white barely showed. The parent eagles may use this breast patch as a gauge to the growing birds immediate food requirement.

The young tiercel had a sleeker, more finished look than his sister. Talon strength of the birds nearly equaled their parents, and for the first time, rabbits were delivered with their fur. Instinctively the young birds pounced and "killed" this game; they squeezed dead rabbits through a "killing" time length. Between the eighth and ninth week, the boy eagle spent more of his day awake than his sister. Much of his time was spent preening and oiling his feathers. Once, while working a wing feather, wind drifting across the aerie caught the young tiercel's open wing. The breeze held his wing weightless. The young bird stopped preening and tentatively opened both wings. They both "flew." For several minutes, he stood with wings outstretched, working his wrist, and changing his leading edge airfoil. The wind died, his wings drooped, and the young eagle returned to preening. From the care and attention he gave his feathers, I suspected the time clock within his system was ticking nearer the day a mysterious force within him would push him into his first flight.

XVIII

YOU HAVE PROBABLY HEARD STORIES about how young eagles make their first flight. Some claim the mother starves the young bird a couple of days, then entices it to fly by cruising in front of the nest with a tantalizing rabbit. Others say the mother carries the fledgling from the nest on her back, then tosses it off to fly or fall. I suppose a myth is better than nothing, but I prefer knowing the truth too. Beginning the ninth week, I spent every free minute I had in the blind. The young female was sixty-four days old, and the young male sixty-two.

While the male preened and groomed, the young lady eagle continued to lay on the nest. She slept a lot, whereas the tiercel sat for long periods, looking out over the canyon. When the wind was right, he held his wings to its lift, sometimes extending them full length. It was then I noticed his wing span, and total feather area was about 10 percent greater than his fathers. I thought on that and concluded that nature provides fledgling eagles with extra wing area. This extra area would lighten the young bird's wing loading. These added square inches of lifting surface would allow young birds to fly slower, making it easier and safer for them to learn to fly. Speed would come to their flight after they molt, in about a year. On his sixty-fourth day, June 8, the young tiercel cautiously stepped into the aerie's landing depression and faced the canyon.

For two days, the tiercel spent hours in the landing depression experimenting with his wings. Sometimes a gust lifted him clear off the nest against his will. Instantly, he deployed spoilers, grabbed nest sticks, and hung on. One day, when the wind was light, I noticed the eagle extend short feathers along the leading edges of his wings, inboard from his wrists. Extending these short feathers altered aerodynamics of his wing in favor of increased lift and/or slower flight speed. On modern jets, these same flight devices are known as Kruger flaps and are deployed for increased lift during relatively slower flight during jet takeoff and landing. Did engineer Kruger learn of this leading edge flap device from eagles? I wondered. At this same time, I observed extra leading edge feathers called *alulae*, outboard from the wrists. These feathers were also used by the young eagle for slow flight. On some aircraft, this same slow flight device is also used, and they are known as slots.

While the young eagle practiced, his sister lay next to the cool rock wall, flat on her tummy, head in his direction. Most of the time she dozed, but occasionally she watched. The young tiercel's practice flight activity increased his appetite, and as near as I could tell, he ate about a pound and a quarter of meat a day. June 9, Her Majesty and Sandose brought two rabbits to the nest. After feeding, the young male preened, napped, and resumed flying practice.

The morning of June 11, his sixty-seventh day of life, the boy eagle rose early. It was warm, with blue sky and a light south wind. The young tiercel stretched, then preened, for half an hour. He worked each feather in each wing and his complete tail fan. Shortly after the youngster finished, Sandose arrived with a half-grown cottontail. The father eagle paused only long enough to grab yesterday's carcass. In a scramble with his sister for the rabbit, the young male won. He ate all of the rodent, including its head, but left the animal's back feet and that small section of intestine. The white patch on his breast showed its maximum.

For the next hour and a half the eagle stood in the landing depression, digesting, touching up his feathers, and surveying the canyon. He seemed especially to study a large boulder a hundred yards to his left, set close to the rock wall and at about a twenty-five–degree angle down.

Across the canyon, a buzzard flew the rim. The young eagle watched. A few minutes later, the mockingbird sailed onto the ledge a few yards away. The little bird eyed the eagle and sang what I guessed was a mocker's opinion of a young eagle sitting on the front edge of an aerie. A fly landed on the eagle's shoulder; however, the bird seemed not to notice. After a long while, the young bird turned his body toward the boulder. A while later, he thrust his head forward and moved his head side to side. The mocker screeched another song. With his eyes on the rock, the young eagle leaned slightly forward and partially opened his wings. After a moment, he closed them. Two or three times, the boy eagle opened and closed his wings. Then he held them open a long moment and let them slowly droop back to the nest. A moment later, the young bird folded his wings, turned his tail toward the canyon, raised his tail fan, and muted.

For half an hour, the young eagle made false starts, each one progressively bolder. At last, he spread his wings, leaned forward, and pushed away with the full force of his legs. His sister raised her head to follow his disappearance. The fledgling dropped away from the aerie and flapped ponderous, desperate wing beats, wavering toward the boulder. Each wing stroke harped the air. Nearing the rock, he awkwardly rotated, stretched his feet, and grabbed. It was here I realized the immature bird was landing with a slight downwind. This downwind nearly doubled his landing speed. The youngster tried to outrun his excessive speed, couldn't, and tumbled on his breast and chin. His tail snapped up, and he skidded to a stop.

The young eagle regained his feet and looked around. Apparently satisfied, he shook his feathers. An instant later, the mockingbird landed on the boulder, a few feet away from the eagle. The fledgling waddled to the rock's highest point and looked at his new surroundings again. The mocker hopped after him. The eagle shook again, and the mocker pranced in back of the eagle. The boy eagle twisted his head and looked at the little bird and turned his eyes to the canyon. Immediately the mocker jumped into the air and kicked its feet squarely in the eagle's back. Quickly the little bird jumped to the rock, a safe distance away. The big bird turned his head to the mocker, looked, and returned his eyes to the canyon. As soon as the eagle's head turned, the mocker pranced up, jumped, and kicked the tiercel's back again. From a safe distance, the little bird squawked at the eagle. The young eagle ignored the tormenter. After a while, the mocker tired of his sport, and left the eagle alone on the boulder.

The mocker wasn't gone more than a minute, however, when the gimpy-footed roadrunner pranced across the canyon floor toward the boulder. As he came near, the cockatoo clacked its beak. At a mesquite nearest the boulder, the prairie bird hopped into low branches and worked its way limb to limb near the tree's top. Here it cocked its head at the eagle, raised and lowered its topknot, clacked, and twitched its tail. I chuckled. The eagle paid little attention. After a while, the roadrunner opened his wings and sailed back to the ground, apparently satisfied at having had his say about an eagle sitting on a boulder. When it was quiet again, the boy eagle preened.

Just after noon, Sandose rose above the rim across the canyon. A prairie dog was in his talons. The fledgling and his sister yee-apped. Sandose started across. Both young eagles continued yee-apping. When the father eagle took the prairie dog to the nest, I guessed he used the bird's white crop patches to make his choice of whom to feed.

For the rest of the day, the boy eagle stayed on the rock, flapping his wings, resting, and preening. Next morning, Sandose crossed the canyon with half a jackrabbit. Again both birds yee-apped. This time, the young male eagle got the food. Sandose paused on the boulder only long enough to release the rabbit. Immediately, the fledgling pounced, "killed," and fed. He then sat in the warming sun, digesting and preening with extra care.

Just after ten o'clock, the fledgling set himself and flew again. The young bird flapped low across the canyon floor, uncertainly dodging larger cedar or mesquite in his flight path. His general heading was toward north rim. From above, a gray Mississippi kite whistled, as though announcing, "Look at this—a young eagle trying his wings! Come on boys, let's have some fun." The little kite sliced toward the tiercel, roared inches above him, pulled up, turned, and dove again. A second kite joined in, and the two took turns dive bombing the awkwardly flapping boy eagle.

The young eagle dropped lower and lower, until he was skimming the prairie between bushes. The kites now rapped the eagle's head with their beaks as they passed, and on pull-up, they shrieked their shrill, whistling call. The boy eagle flapped across the stream. Against the rising ground, he began trying to land, more from necessity than from planning. The wind was a quartering downwind, which would again add speed to his touch down. The angling wind caused him to slue across the ground. He fought the slue and speed by grabbing at buffalo grass tufts passing beneath. At last he touched down and came to a comical stop on his belly, with his wings spread on the ground. His right leg stretched behind; his talons clutched a short tuft of grass and earth. A kite roared above the eagle's head and rapped his crown sharply.

The boy eagle gathered himself, stood, and shook. Dust filled air around him, and the eagle's first two landings convinced me the birds must learn about wind and its effects on flight. Sandose flew from his guard post and slowly angled along the rim, nearer. The fledgling yee-apped, and so did his sister from across the canyon. The kites returned to their aerial locust and dragonfly catching. Sandose made only a short flight and landed on the rim. The young eagles hushed. After a few minutes, the immature male eagle started walking toward north rim.

For forty-five minutes the eagle walked, rested, and walked again. At the base of the canyon wall, the young eagle leaned forward into the increased rise and walked on. With the tips of his primary's crossed across his rump, he looked like an elderly gentleman walking stooped. At the edge of a house-sized boulder, he half-flapped and half-hopped up on its low side. After resting, he waddled to the boulder's highest point. Here he preened again, working all of his primaries and all of his tail fan. On the cliff above, Sandose watched.

The wind remained light. It was updraft here, and during wing preening, the boy eagle sometimes let the breeze catch his wing. Once he finished working his feathers, he faced into the canyon and into the wind, spread his wings, and lifted.

The young eagle rose, at the same time drifting toward the cliff behind. On unsteady wings, he experimented with airfoil and tail fan settings in search of a mode that would hold the wind from dashing him against the cliff yet would keep him afloat. At what seemed like certain collision with the rock wall, he made a lurching turn. The wind continued carrying him lightly up the cliff, and suddenly, he was above the rim, flying free.

Almost immediately, Sandose was next to him. The young eagle yee-apped, and yee-apped, almost sounding as if he was yelling "Help, help!" Her Majesty joined them. The wide white band in his tail fan and the white patches at his wrist joints stood out like neon signs. The young bird tried to hover, but his flight was unsteady. I was amused at the amount of space his parents kept between them and their newly airborne son. The bird's cries subsided, and he settled into further experimenting. He was slow in compensating for slight changes in updraft or wind drifts. As a result, his altitude and position were erratic, and he rose, or dropped above and below his stabilized parents. Quickly, however, his flight improved, and I wondered how long he would stay up. I was also curious as to where his next landing would be and how it would turn out.

After half an hour's flying with his parents, the young eagle eased toward the rim. Above its edge, he maneuvered to land. His reflexes were still behind changes in the wind. He grabbed at the rock and settled onto the rim, almost gracefully. Her Majesty landed next to him. Sandose eased over his guard post and alighted. The three birds sat for fifteen or twenty minutes in the heating sun. At last, the adults flew across the canyon, and perched on a shaded ledge. The young male bird walked along the rim, to the shade of a cedar rooted on the canyon's edge. It was late evening before he flew again.

Just before sunset, the young man eagle spread his wings and rose. The cooler air was smoother, and that's how he flew. At first, he simply rose, slowly descended, and rose again. Once in a while, he tentatively turned, as though considering a circle. After a few false starts, he finally banked from the rim and made a rocky, not perfect, hurried circle. Facing back into the canyon, he rose, hesitated, and circled again. This time he was more precise, and his confidence showed. Soon after he learned to circle reasonably well, he discovered if he paralleled the rim, and nosed down a little to compensate for updraft, his speed was fast. At sundown, he was making short speed dashes along the rim, then rising into a circle and descending into a new speed run back where he had come from. When it was almost dark, the fledgling still flew speed dashes and circles, almost like a kid with a new toy just before bedtime. When it became too dark for further flight, he landed near the cedar he had used for shade, waddled under the tree, and settled for the night.

Early the next morning Her Majesty and Sandose were in the air over north rim. Both young eagles yee-apped from their different locations. The young man eagle spread his wings and joined his parents in the air. He continued crying to them, but quieted when the adults sailed away to hunt. The young bird rose, until he was probably four or five hundred feet. From here, he watched his parents. About a quarter of a mile away, Her Majesty flushed a rabbit. Sandose caught it. Immediately, the boy eagle backed his wings and streaked toward them. Nearing them, his speed was excessive; he was on a quartering tailwind. Uncertainly, he rocked his wings into a turn that carried him past them and brought him about for landing into the wind. Obviously, the youngster had learned the basic principles of flight. I smiled.

Her Majesty and Sandose stood aside for their son. He landed on the rabbit. It is possible the rabbit wasn't quite dead, but it made no difference—the young male killed it anyway and fed.

The rest of the day, the young tiercel flew and rested. On one flight, a sparrow hawk harassed him, driving him lower and lower. At last the young eagle turned on his back in midair and slashed talons at the little hawk. From then on, the sparrow hawk didn't come so close, and the fledgling eagle didn't yield altitude to its harassment. At this point, I returned my attention to the young girl eagle in the nest.

The day the girl eagle started the routine of preflight preening and flapping practice in the landing depression, she was exactly eleven weeks and two days old. Her wingspan was two inches short of eight feet, and she weighed eight and a half pounds. Her nearly black color, banded tail, white-wristed wings, large head, large beak, large talons, and heavy-browed eyes gave her a formidable look. The fact that her schedule followed the male by almost two weeks raised my curiosity. I came to this conclusion: Since her size is greater, it probably takes this much more time to develop and strengthen her wing bones to withstand the stress of flight. I also now understand why some observers have recorded that young eagles fledge in nine weeks, while others said up to twelve.

The third morning of her preen and practice was cool for June 23. Wind was moderately strong from north. It was the eighty-first day of the young girl eagle's life, or only three days short of twelve weeks. The wind gusted straight into the nest. A couple of hours after sunrise, Her Majesty brought a half-grown cotton-tail. The wind made her landing difficult. A few minutes later, Sandose came with a tiny ground squirrel. He also found flying near and into the nest difficult. Although the young girl eagle's white crop patch showed well after she fed, she probably wasn't full. But I was sure she wasn't starved, either. For a while after feeding, she stood next to the nest's wall, out of the wind, and preened. Just after noon, she stepped into the landing depression. Sometimes the wind ruffled one of her feathers. After hesitating a moment, she spread her wings and started to flap, as she had done yesterday. Instantly, she was airborne. Desperately, she reached for the nest with her long legs. A gust lifted her higher. Her feet were down, and I sensed her becoming airborne was an accident. A new gust shoved her to within a millimeter of throwing her against the cliff. I scrambled from the blind. With her ponderous wings rocking, she brought her feet up and was rapidly borne by the wind to the rim and a hundred feet above. Within seconds, she was two hundred feet, then three hundred. Sandose sailed in from no where and stabilized fairly close to her. The young girl eagle yee-apped and yee-apped. A moment later, Her Majesty arrived, and the adults flew a spaced formation on their child's unsteady flight. Her size was truly awesome, larger than her mother's, and I could hear the echo of someone who would have said they had just seen "the biggest eagle you ever saw in your life." I climbed to the rim as fast as I could.

On top, the wind was less than at its interface with the cliff. The eagles moved upcanyon, away from me, and Sandose hunted. Her Majesty hesitated in leaving the young girl eagle before joining Sandose. A third of a mile back from the rim, Sandose caught something, but I couldn't be sure what. Immediately the young eagle slanted into a dive that was fast, considering her

experience; but it was probably not more than fifty miles per
hour through the air. However, she sailed downwind, giving her
a ground speed of close to sixty-five. A couple of hundred yards
from Sandose, she slowed, but only a little. Apprehension rose
within me. At a hundred yards, she was still too fast. My apprehension mushroomed. At fifty yards, she was in trouble but
didn't seem to know. In a flash, I remembered a gunnery practice
phenomenon fighter pilots experience called *target fixation*. Target fixation lures an afflicted pilot to fly right into the target he
is shooting at. The girl eagle dove on, lower and lower. As she
neared Sandose, the prairie rushed under her wings rapidly. Sandose jumped aside.

At the last possible second, the girl eagle tried to rotate her
feet forward. But she was too late. Her body slammed into the
ground just beyond Sandose. In a cloud of dust and a flurry of
feathers, the young eagle tumbled end over end across the prairie.
When she stopped, she flopped in the grass, gyrating like a headless chicken. Then, she became quiet and she lay still. Wind lifted
a wing from behind. There was no life in the wing. I hurried to
the young girl eagle. The fledgling female eagle's neck was
broken. As I carried her body to my car, I realized nature is sometimes cruel, too.

Soon after learning to handle his sparrow hawk problem, the
boy eagle made his first solo hunt. By mid-July, he had learned
to catch some game on his own. During one of these solo hunts,
he strayed across the territory line and got his first lesson in
remaining on his side. At the same time, he got a close look at
the girl eagle the neighboring pair were fledgling.

In August, the eagle's territory instincts diminished, and the
Texas canyon eagle population became reasonably sociable. The
birds penetrated each others territory with little more than token
opposition. In a short time, the boy and girl eagle hunted together,
sometimes over one territory, sometimes over the other, without

interference from adult eagles. I wasn't able to see if the young birds shared their catches or not, but I did see them on different days playing drop-and-catch-the-rock.

Sometimes the four adult eagles ranged two or three miles beyond either family's home grounds. On these trips, I wondered if the parent eagles were scouting areas their offspring might be encouraged to establish, in anticipation of a day that seemed to be coming.

The canyon's cottonwood turned to gold. Sparrow hawks migrated away, and a few early ducks paddled in pools along the stream. Late in November, Her Majesty felt the first twinges of her seasonal nesting urge. One afternoon, just after Thanksgiving, she and Sandose gently steered their young man eagle beyond flat-top bush. When the young bird tried to come back, his parents used firm flight tactics to keep him out. At first the young eagle seemed confused, and his return attempts developed into juvenile determination. Sandose's and Her Majesty's determination matched the youngster's, and after a while, the immature eagle reduced his attempts. On occasion, and at high altitude, the adult birds let the young eagle back over the land of his birth. However, he was never allowed to hunt or to linger. Then, in January, Her Majesty and Sandose closed their border. About this same time, the young man tiercel eagle and the young girl eagle became established grooming and hunting partners. Their life expectancy is fifty to a hundred years.

The question of why female eagles are larger than males continued to bother me. I guess I was gnawed because I wasn't satisfied with my original theory. One January day in front of the fire, it occurred that maybe I had asked the question backwards. Maybe the question should be: Why are male eagles smaller than female eagles?

Obviously, the tiercel, as territory defender, must be the faster, more nimble partner. As fighter plane in the family, he must be designed like a fighter plane. From my flying experience, smaller and lighter fits. Here I paused and noted the difference between land creature and air creature requirements for territory defense; for example, the bulk of a bull elephant, the mass of a male lion, the hulk of a boar bear. In the sky, however, bulk, mass, and hulk yield to agility and speed. The flash of a fighter plane dominates the sluggishness of a bomber. I nodded my head, more certain I had been asking the question backwards.

Then I realized, if my theory is near the mark, male sharks should be smaller than female sharks, because in water, smaller is also faster and more agile. I rose and checked my natural history reference books. No mention. I phoned the Amarillo library's reference department and asked my question.

Male sharks are smaller than female sharks. And male bass are smaller than their mates, and the same goes for guppies. My mind relaxed. I was satisfied as to why nature designed male eagles smaller than female eagles.

After "True Nature" showings of my eagle film, fellow workers and fans asked how I got interested in the king of birds in the first place. The question startled. I had been so busy watching, I hadn't thought about it. So, I took time to think.

I suppose my initial attraction to the eagle was the birds' grace and beauty in flight, the way they soared with the delicacy of a butterfly one minute then sliced the sky with the authority of a fighter bomber the next. I'm also impressed with the eagles' command over their lives. That may spring from a secret yearning of my own, as a human caught in modern society. And as I learned of the eagles' dependency on each other (for hunting, grooming, and sex) I guess I related. Also, way back in my mind, I think I even look to the eagle as a bellwether: "If the eagle can't make it in the twentieth century, can we?"

The more I compared the human being to the eagle, the more I am convinced the birds are models of pair bond life-style, ego ideals if you will. Even so, there remain unanswered questions about the birds. For example, is the splotched egg always male and the cream female? Motion along the canyon rim caught my eye. I went to the window. Sandose and Her Majesty were forcing an American eagle to high altitude. Once there, the pair flew in escort formation on the American, across their territory. Where do the American eagles that migrate to Palo Duro Canyon come from? I wondered. And how do their lives compare with the golden eagle? I left the fire and dressed for another day in the canyon.

EPILOGUE

SINCE WRITING *A Family of Eagles,* I may have accidentally discovered an easier solution to the Cain-Abel batle. From a nest in Cooley Draw on the Elkins Ranch, adjacent to Currie, I took the younger eaglet as soon as the fight erupted, before significant damage was done. My intent was to feed the little bird at a clip equal to its nestmate, and hope that within a few days the smaller bird would be able to fend for itself. After three days I put the bird back and watched.

When the mother eagle returned, I saw both eaglets snuggle under her. Next day, I was amazed to see that the battle was never resumed. I decided the older chick may have had a one-way tape in its inherited programming. Possibly when the "threat" to its territory was removed, the larger eaglet's brain recorded "Threat gone . . . life is normal." It is possible that when the little chick returns after an extended absence, the older chick's tape keeps going forward and doesn't rewind to "threat." Just a theory. However, when I test it, I will take the oldest bird out for a couple of days while leaving the younger one in its mother's care. I will do so on the presumption that the bird with mother probably gets superior care and feeding.

Regarding a possible correlation between the sex of golden eagle chicks and the splotchiness, or plainness, of eggs they hatch from, I posed the question to Mr. James W. Grier, Laboratory of Ornithology, Cornell University. Mr. Grier replied: "I would not expect sex to depend on the splotchiness of the egg for two reasons:

1) I cannot imagine any selective advantage that would have led to the evolution of such a correlation, and 2) even if there were an advantage to it, I think the process of (the mother eagle) detecting the sex of the fertilized ova and then applying the proper pigment in the shell gland would be beyond the physiological capabilities of the female eagle's reproductive system."

A few months after Her Majesty and Sandose finished the nesting season, Randall County Sheriff Cliff Longest came to my home with a dead eagle. Sheriff Longest said a farmer saw the bird electrocuted on a transformer pole along FM 2177, between Canyon, Texas and Palo Duro State Park, or a few miles south of Currie Ranch. The eagle was banded. I read its number and checked my records. The bird was Sandose.

Sadly, I wrapped him in a trash bag and placed the bag in a freezer. Later, the eagle's carcass was picked up by a federal game official, who explained that the eagle's feathers would be removed and sent to the National Eagle Repository in Pocatello, Idaho. From there, Sandose's feather would be distributed to reservation Indians who still use the eagle, or parts thereof, in tribal religious rites. This enables Indians to use feathers from dead birds, rather than having to kill one, which they may legally do.

The flight device of spoilers is apparently more common in the bird world than I imagined. I have seen English sparrows deploy spoilers in some landings on city sidewalks. I have also discovered that these devices are simple to see in most any eagle or hawk film in movies or on television. If the scene is filmed at the right angle, you can spot spoiler and/or Kruger flap deployment just as the birds land.

As for Douglas, he didn't resume falconry after his military service. For a time, he was part of the stage crew for the rock group Black Oak Arkansas. Later, he operated heavy machinery on the Texas South plains. At last report, he was a roughneck on an oil drilling rig in western Oklahoma.

The next year, for whatever reason, the eggs of the Cooley Draw pair were sterile. After forty-seven days, nothing. At that same time, a Texas Parks and Wildlife official brought an eight-to ten-day old eaglet confiscated from a nest robber. The official asked that I raise the youngster. I decided real eagles make better parents than I, so I placed the eaglet in the Cooley Draw nest. At the same time I removed one of the apparently sterile eggs. (It was.) From a distance, I watched. After the hen eagle returned to the nest, she hesitated, then resettled on her egg. The eaglet screamed a long while; however, there was no food on the nest. At the time I overlooked the food detail, else I would have provided it. At last the little bird snuggled under its foster mother without incident. Next day, however, I found the chick dead on the edge of the nest. A small portion of the eaglet's intestine protruded from its anus, as though the little bird had been squeezed beyond endurance. In addition, the chick's body bore a couple of small indentations similar to the kind Sandose put on my arm the last day I played falconer. My guess is that the tiercel may have killed the chick when he came to take his turn brooding. I'm guessing the male bird may have regarded the screaming eaglet as an intruder into his territory. I'm further guessing that since the hen eagle had no opportunity to "talk" to the eaglet as it hatched, she had no rapport with the newcomer. Without that rapport, she apparently felt no bond, and may have left the nest in charge of the tiercel while she went to hunt. Natural mother eagles I've observed have never left their chicks alone with the tiercel when the eaglets were small.

On a trip through Rosewell, New Mexico, where there are plenty of both sheep and wintering eagles, as well as much controversy about that combination, I paused one September afternoon to talk with taxidermist George D. Hamrick. I asked George his opinion about the eagle-lamb controversy. He smiled and said that in 1917–18, he worked as a hand on the Three S's

Ranch north of Petersburg, Texas. George said that they raised many lambs and there were many eagles, but no problem between the two. He volunteered that in his opinion, there was no problem until sheep ranchers recognized the value of tax advantages inherent to "lamb losses" to eagles. I then asked how his view might set with local sheep ranchers. He shrugged, and pointed out that he was old enough to be past worrying over what people thought of his estimations.

In summer, after the young eagles fledge, the birds are more difficult to watch because they spend most of the day in the shade. Hunting is done around sunrise and sunset. Both times conflicted with my television schedule, so I have little summer data. I'm leading to this: The eagles are sexually active from late December to June . . . six months. That probably qualifies the birds as second only to humans in sexual activity. Unanswered, however, is the question of the eagle's sex life through summer and early fall.

Regarding the male-female eagle's size differential, I called my sophomore-college-year roommate John Berwick, now Cessna Aircraft's single-engine division chief engineer. I gave John the wing span and weight of a tiercel, and asked how much larger that bird's wing area and body weight should be to accommodate the extra load a female carries prior to egg laying. He ran the figures through his slide rule and estimated that twenty percent larger should be about right. Female eagles are about twenty percent larger and heavier than males.

American eagle migration into Palo Duro Canyon remains a mystery. This I know: The birds arrive on a day in October, November, or December, when surface winds are strong westerly, and forty- to sixty-mph winds are aloft over Albuquerque, Denver, El Paso, and Amarillo. To get an eagle's slide ratio, I called Ed Blick at Oklahoma University's Aeronautical Engineering School. Ed estimated that with those winds, an eagle would need an altitude of around sixteen thousand feet to glide to Palo Duro Canyon without flapping a feather. Sixteen thousand feet would be less than six thousand feet above Sandia Mountain at Albuquerque. Strong interfacing mountain winds would lift an eagle six thousand feet above the ridge in two to three minutes. From there, a trip to the canyon would take about two hours. The American eagle's migration month seems to hinge on when the lakes in Colorado and New Mexico freeze. (The birds take fish from these lakes.) I think the birds ride the Rocky Mountain waves from Alaska and Canada to New Mexico.

I have data from two occasions on the hour the birds left Palo Duro in the spring. On both occasions, panhandle winds were drifting from east to west, toward New Mexico. One year I secured telephone permission from federal game people to notch a *V* into the tail feathers of as many American eagles as I could so mark. However, I was asked to wait before acting until I received written confirmation. Time was running out for that year, so one dusk in late March, Douglas and I checked the three main American eagle perch areas on Currie Ranch. Over twenty birds were in the canyon. Early next morning, I buried Douglas in canyon sands away from our golden eagles and tied a pigeon on his belly. We waited until noon, with no action, before giving up for the day. That afternoon, my written permission arrived. At dusk we rechecked perches. The birds were gone.

Since that spring, I haven't had a chance to try to mark American eagles. But some day, I will.